BIBLE
PUZZLES
for Girls

BARBOUR
PUBLISHING

ISBN 978-1-62416-731-7

All scripture quotations are taken from the King James Version of the Bible.

Published by Barbour Publishing, Inc., P.O. Box 719, Uhrichsville, Ohio 44683 www.barbourbooks.com

Our mission is to publish and distribute inspirational products offering exceptional value and biblical encouragement to the masses.

ecpa Member of the
Evangelical Christian
Publishers Association

Printed in the United States of America.
Bethany Press International, Bloomington, MN 55438; January 2014;
D10004299

 # Contents

Welcome to Bible Puzzles for Girls!

The Bible is jam-packed with exciting stories that girls love—from the creation of Eve to the courageous Queen Esther, from Jesus' amazing miracles to young Rhoda's funny encounter with the apostle Peter. In the pages to follow, you'll find dozens of word search and crossword puzzles to test your knowledge of each story!

Perfect for kids ages 7–10, *Bible Puzzles for Girls* provides hours of good, clean fun. Best of all, you'll be learning more and more about God's Word, the Bible. What could be better than that?

All Bible quotations are taken from the classic King James Version of scripture—and all answers will be in the King James spelling. Have a Bible (or a Bible web site) handy when you solve the puzzles. . .that's okay, it's not cheating! The whole idea is to get you deeper into God's Word.

When you work the word search puzzles, look for bold words in the Bible passage—they're the ones you'll find in the puzzle grid. If the words are bold and underlined, they'll appear together in the puzzle grid.

For added fun, you'll find some amazing trivia questions sprinkled throughout. Puzzle answers begin on page 177, while the trivia answers are set upside down below each question.

Have fun!

1. Creation
GENESIS 1:1–31

ACROSS

5. What God did "in the beginning" (v. 1)

6. What else did God create besides male? (v. 27)

8. One of the things man is to "have dominion" (rule) over (v. 26)

9. The lights in the firmament (sky) are to mark years and what else? (v. 14)

DOWN

1. The day God called the firmament Heaven (sky) (v. 8)

2. Who created the heaven and the earth? (v. 1)

3. What else did God create besides female? (v. 27)

4. God created man using His what as an example? (v. 26)

6. The day God created "Day" and "Night" (v. 5)

7. Another name for "Earth" (v. 10)

2. The Very First Woman
GENESIS 2:18–24

And the LORD God said, It is not good that the man should be alone; I will make him an help meet for him. And out of the ground the LORD God formed every beast of the field, and every fowl of the air; and brought them unto Adam to see what he would call them: and whatsoever Adam called every living creature, that was the name thereof. And Adam gave names to all cattle, and to the fowl of the air, and to every beast of the field; but for Adam there was not found an help meet for him. And the LORD God caused a **deep sleep** to fall upon Adam, and he slept: and he took one of his **ribs**, and **closed** up the flesh instead thereof; and the rib, which the LORD God had taken from man, made he a woman, and brought her unto the man. And Adam said, This is now **bone** of my bones, and **flesh** of my flesh: she shall be called **Woman**, because she was taken out of Man. Therefore shall a man **leave** his father and his mother, and shall cleave unto his **wife**: and they shall be one flesh.

```
R E R T C Y U I O P
M I N B V L E A V E
W C B J E N O N V A
W O D O S A W B S D Y
M E N M F S G M E R
A P E E L S P E E D
N S V B E X T J U E
K Y T G S C R A F S
J P L E H V F I K T
F O R M E D W O U Y
```

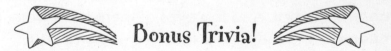

Bonus Trivia!

How did Jacob describe his brother, Esau?

a) scary
b) wary
c) hairy
d) merry

3. Sneaky Snake
GENESIS 3:1–7

Now the **serpent** was more subtil than any beast of the field which the LORD God had made. And he said unto the **woman**, Yea, hath God said, Ye shall not eat of every tree of the **garden**? And the woman said unto the serpent, We may eat of the fruit of the trees of the garden: But of the fruit of the tree which is in the **midst** of the garden, God hath said, Ye shall not eat of it, neither shall ye touch it, lest ye die. And the serpent said unto the woman, Ye shall not surely **die**: For God doth know that in the day ye eat thereof, then your eyes shall be opened, and ye shall be as gods, knowing **good** and evil. And when the woman saw that the **tree** was good for food, and that it was pleasant to the **eyes**, and a tree to be desired to make one **wise**, she took of the **fruit** thereof, and did eat, and gave also unto her husband with her; and he did eat. And the eyes of them both were **opened**, and they knew that they were naked; and they sewed **fig leaves** together, and made themselves aprons.

```
A S F D G J H K L P
G A R D E N O I S D
O Y U E T R W E S E
O M I D S T V E V N
D D T M B A R W N E
Z X C R E P V O B P
N S G L E H W M J O
K R G N Y E I A T W
X I T P E O S N I U
F A R E S V E M K O
```

4. A Boat Full of Animals
GENESIS 7:1–10

ACROSS

1. The number of days and nights in this story (v. 4)

3. The person God talked with (v. 1)

6. Number of clean animals this person should take (v. 2)

DOWN

1. What covered the earth (v. 10)

2. What was going to fall on the earth (v. 4)

4. The purpose for taking in some of the animals (v. 3)

5. The type animals that Noah took seven of (v. 2)

6. The boat builder was this many hundred years old (v. 6)

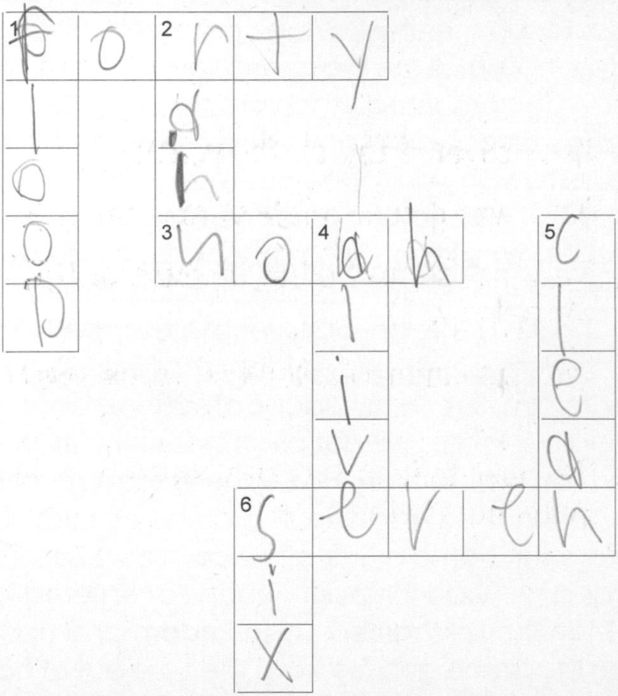

5. Turned into a Salt Statue
GENESIS 19:15–26

And when the morning arose, then the angels hastened Lot, saying, Arise, take thy **wife**, and thy two daughters, which are here; lest thou be consumed in the iniquity of the city. And while he lingered, the men laid hold upon his hand, and upon the hand of his wife, and upon the hand of his two daughters; the LORD being merciful unto him: and they brought him forth, and set him without the city. And it came to pass, when they had brought them forth abroad, that he said, **Escape** for thy life; look not behind thee, neither stay thou in all the plain; escape to the mountain, lest thou be consumed. And **Lot** said unto them, Oh, not so, my Lord: Behold now, thy servant hath found grace in thy sight, and thou hast magnified thy mercy, which thou hast shewed unto me in saving my life; and I cannot escape to the mountain, lest some evil take me, and I die: Behold now, this city is near to flee unto, and it is a little one: Oh, let me escape thither, (is it not a little one?) and my soul shall live. And he said unto him, See, I have accepted thee concerning this thing also, that I will not overthrow this city, for the which thou hast spoken. Haste thee, escape thither; for I cannot do anything till thou be come thither. Therefore the name of the city was called Zoar. The sun was risen upon the earth when Lot entered into Zoar. Then the LORD **rained** upon **Sodom** and upon **Gomorrah** brimstone and **fire** from the LORD out of **heaven**; and he overthrew those cities, and all the plain, and all the inhabitants of the cities, and that which grew upon the ground. But his wife **looked back** from behind him, and she became a **pillar** of **salt**.

```
K I H E A V E N F L
C U L M E G Z L M K
A Y P F L O T O R J
B T I K Q M D R T D
D W L N A O X D E H
E R L B S R S N E G
K S A L T R I V R F
O E R C V A W C I D
O W Z X R H E D F S
L Q E P A C S E G A
```

6. An Extremely Old Couple Have Their First Baby
GENESIS 21:1–8

And the LORD visited Sarah as he had said, and the **LORD** did unto Sarah as he had spoken. For **Sarah** conceived, and bare Abraham a **son** in his **old** age, at the set time of which God had spoken to him. And Abraham called the name of his son that was born unto him, whom Sarah bare to him, Isaac. And Abraham circumcised his son **Isaac** being **eight** days old, as God had commanded him. And Abraham was an **hundred** years old, when his son Isaac was born unto him. And Sarah said, God hath made me to **laugh**, so that all that hear will laugh with me. And she said, Who would have said unto **Abraham**, that Sarah should have given children suck? for I have born him a son in his old age. And the child **grew**, and was **weaned**: and Abraham made a great **feast** the same day that Isaac was weaned.

```
M U A W E R G T R Z
A J R E K O T S F A
H M S A I S A A C Q
A U O N I M H R V X
R K N E E G Y A T S
B I P D U N L H S W
A L O A R H O E A C
N B L V C E R G E Z
T R E W O L D Q F M
E I G H T P O I U Y
```

Bonus Trivia!

Where did the prophet Jonah spend three strange days and nights?

 a) on a spaceship
 b) in an eagle's nest
 c) under a waterfall
 d) inside a fish

Answer: d) inside a fish (Jonah 1:17)

7. God Loves and Helps Children

GENESIS 21:14–21

And Abraham rose up early in the morning, and took bread, and a bottle of water, and gave it unto Hagar, putting it on her shoulder, and the child, and sent her away: and she departed, and **wandered** in the wilderness of **Beersheba**. And the water was spent in the bottle, and she cast the child under one of the shrubs. And she went, and sat her down over against him a good way off, as it were a bow shot: for she said, Let me not see the death of the child. And she sat over against him, and lift up her voice, and wept. And God **heard** the voice of the lad; and the **angel** of God called to **Hagar** out of heaven, and said unto her, What aileth thee, Hagar? fear not; for God hath heard the voice of the lad where he is. Arise, lift up the lad, and hold him in thine hand; for I will make him a great **nation**. And God **opened** her **eyes**, and she saw a **well** of water; and she went, and filled the bottle with **water**, and gave the lad **drink**. And God was with the lad; and he grew, and dwelt in the wilderness, and became an **archer**. And he dwelt in the wilderness of Paran: and his mother took him a wife out of the land of Egypt.

L D X A R C H E R L
K M R E L L E W O N
J A T I Y T T A I O
H A C O N E Q N U I
W S V P L K S D J T
H B E E R S H E B A
A D G N O Y W R M N
G N B E P U E E H P
A F N D Z I R D N S
R G H E A R D G B A

8. Nations in a Tummy
GENESIS 25:20–28

ACROSS

    2. A description of the first baby was (v. 25)

    4. The color of the first baby was (v. 25)

    5. The name of the first baby (v. 25)

    7. The place where two nations were (v. 23)

DOWN

    1. What this mother was originally (v. 21)

    2. Part of his brother the younger twin grabbed (v. 26)

    3. Name of the second baby (v. 26)

    6. Number of nations in the mother's womb (v. 23)

Bonus Trivia!

What color horse does Jesus ride during the great battle in the book of Revelation?

    a) gold

    b) red

    c) white

    d) black

Answer: c) white (Revelation 19:11)

9. Dad Forces Sisters to Trick Future Husband

Genesis 29:15–30

ACROSS

3. Name of the father who tricked Jacob (v. 25)

5. Number of daughters the father had (v. 16)

6. Name of the older daughter (v. 16)

8. Time of day the wedding took place (v. 23)

DOWN

1. What the father asked of Jacob, so he would not work for free (v. 15)

2. Name of the daughter Jacob loved more (v. 30)

4. What was not to be given in marriage before the firstborn (v. 26)

7. Number of years Jacob worked to earn his bride (v. 30)

10. Baby Floating in a River
Exodus 2:1–10

ACROSS

    4. The person brought to care for the baby (v. 8)

    5. What the baby was drawn out of (v. 10)

    6. What the baby became to the Egyptian who found him (v. 10)

    7. Purpose for calling the baby's mother (v. 7)

DOWN

    1. The family member of Pharaoh who came to the river (v. 5)

    2. The nationality of the baby and its mother (v. 7)

    3. The baby's family member who called the mother (v. 7)

    4. Name of the baby (v. 10)

11. Moses and the Family
Exodus 2:16–22

Now the priest of **Midian** had **seven** daughters: and they came and drew water, and filled the **troughs** to water their father's flock. And the shepherds came and drove them away: but **Moses** stood up and helped them, and **watered** their **flock**. And when they came to **Reuel** their father, he said, How is it that ye are come so soon to day? And they said, An Egyptian delivered us out of the hand of the shepherds, and also drew water enough for us, and watered the flock. And he said unto his daughters, And where is he? why is it that ye have left the man? call him, that he may eat **bread**. And Moses was **content** to dwell with the man: and he gave Moses **Zipporah** his daughter. And she bare him a **son**, and he called his name **Gershom**: for he said, I have been a stranger in a strange land.

S	P	L	O	K	I	M	J	U	N
H	G	E	R	S	H	O	M	J	Z
G	D	A	E	R	B	W	O	K	I
U	M	I	D	I	A	N	S	C	P
O	U	N	H	T	Y	B	E	O	P
R	G	N	E	T	V	F	S	L	O
T	S	R	E	R	C	D	E	F	R
D	E	O	X	V	S	U	W	Z	A
D	C	O	N	T	E	N	T	A	H
Q	K	I	U	R	F	S	E	S	A

Bonus Trivia!

What made King Saul stand out from the rest of the Israelites?

- a) He was stronger.
- b) He had darker skin.
- c) He was taller.
- d) He had a nicer voice.

Answer: c) He was taller (1 Samuel 9:2)

29

12. Miracle Food in the Desert

Exodus 16:1–31

ACROSS

2. Who promised to feed the people? (v. 4)

4. Birds that came and covered the camp (v. 13)

5. Food God promised to send from heaven (v. 4)

8. Amount to be gathered on the sixth day (v. 22)

9. Name of the wilderness desert (v. 1)

DOWN

1. What the miracle food looked like on the ground (v. 14)

3. Name the people gave to the miracle food (v. 15)

6. How the food was to come down from heaven (v. 4)

7. What lay around the camp in the morning (v. 13)

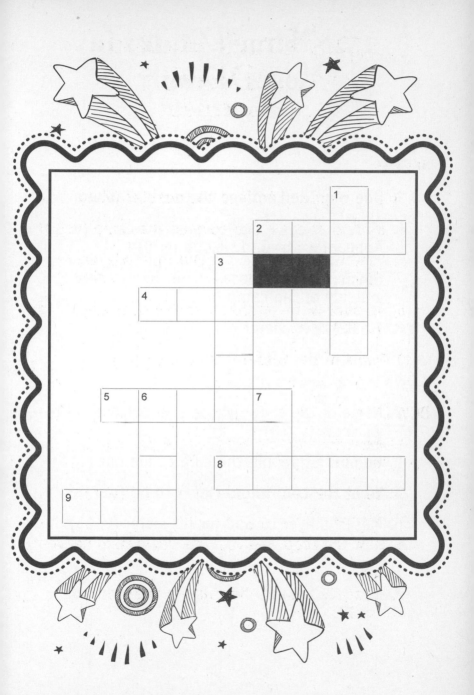

13. Sibling Rivalry in Moses' Family

Numbers 12:1–16

ACROSS

1. One way the Lord speaks to His prophets (v. 6)

5. Appearance of God's cloud (v. 5)

7. Number of days Moses' sister had to stay outside of the camp (v. 14)

8. What Moses' sister became (v. 10)

DOWN

2. Name of the sister whose skin became white as snow (v. 10)

3. Number of people the Lord called out (v. 4)

4. What the Lord found Moses to be (v. 7)

6. Moses' prayer to God for his sister (v. 13)

14. A Talking Donkey!

NUMBERS 22:21–38

ACROSS

    2. What the donkey turned aside into (v. 23)

    3. What the donkey's rider did when he saw the angel (v. 31)

    6. Width of the pathway (v. 26)

    7. Number of times the rider hit his donkey (v. 28)

DOWN

    1. Where the walls were (v. 24)

    3. Name of the man riding the donkey (v. 21)

    4. What the Lord did with the rider's eyes (v. 31)

    5. What the angel held in his hand (v. 31)

    7. Number of servants with the donkey rider (v. 22)

15. A Woman Helps Spies
Joshua 2:1–7

ACROSS

2. Place on the house where the woman brought the spies (v. 6)

3. Name of the man who sent out the spies (v. 1)

4. What the woman hid the spies under (v. 6)

6. River near the woman's city (v. 7)

DOWN

1. Number of men sent to spy (v. 1)

2. Name of the woman who helped hide the spies (v. 1)

3. Name of the city the woman lived in (v. 1)

5. What the spies were sent to look over, view, and spy on (v. 1)

16. Daughter Asks Daddy for a Gift

JUDGES 1:11–20

And from thence he went against the inhabitants of Debir: and the name of Debir before was Kirjathsepher: And **Caleb** said, He that smiteth Kirjathsepher, and taketh it, to him will I give Achsah my **daughter** to wife. And **Othniel** the son of Kenaz, Caleb's **younger** brother, took it: and he gave him Achsah his daughter to wife. And it came to pass, when she came to him, that she moved him to ask of her father a **field**: and she lighted from off her ass; and Caleb said unto her, What wilt thou? And she said unto him, Give me a **blessing**: for thou hast given me a south land; give me also springs of water. And Caleb gave her the upper springs and the nether **springs**. And the children of the Kenite, Moses' father in law, went up out of the city of **palm** trees with the children of Judah into the wilderness of Judah, which lieth in the south of Arad; and they went and dwelt among the people. And Judah went with Simeon his brother, and they slew the Canaanites that inhabited Zephath, and utterly destroyed it. And the name of the city was called Hormah. Also Judah took Gaza with the coast thereof, and Askelon with the coast thereof, and Ekron with the coast thereof. And the LORD was with Judah; and he drave out the inhabitants of the mountain; but could not drive out the inhabitants of the valley, because they had chariots of **iron**. And they gave **Hebron** unto Caleb, as Moses said: and he expelled thence the **three** sons of Anak.

```
S F R T L O R D G B
P E E R H T D L C V
R D A U G H T E R R
I A Z X S N W I E E
N V C X Z I Q F H G
G N I S S E L B E N
S P M R N L E B B U
G F A D O L S A R O
Q L K L A N J H O Y
I U Y C M T R E N W
```

17. The Lady Judge and the Heroine
JUDGES 4:4–23

ACROSS

1. Place Sisera fled to (v. 17)

4. Name of the lady who judged Israel (v. 4)

6. What the heroine gave Sisera instead of water (v. 19)

7. How the heroine found Sisera (v. 21)

DOWN

1. Name of the mountain where the battle occurred (v. 14)

2. What Sisera did on foot (v. 17)

3. Name of the heroine (v. 17)

5. What the heroine used to pound a peg through Sisera's temple (v. 21)

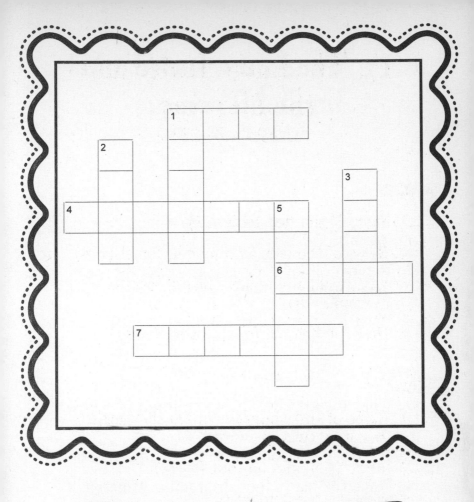

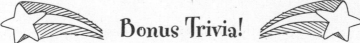

Bonus Trivia!

Who is Michael in the New Testament?

    a) a disciple of Jesus

    b) a Roman governor

    c) an archangel

    d) the author of Galatians

18. A Man, a Girl, and a Very Foolish Promise

JUDGES 11:29–40

ACROSS

3. Name of the man who made a foolish promise (v. 30)

6. Number of days per year the daughters of Israel lament (v. 40)

7. What the man did to the Lord (v. 30)

DOWN

1. What the man did to the children of Ammon (v. 33)

2. The girl's relationship to the man (v. 34)

4. Place the man's foolish promise affected (v. 31)

5. Number of months the girl asked to be alone (v. 37)

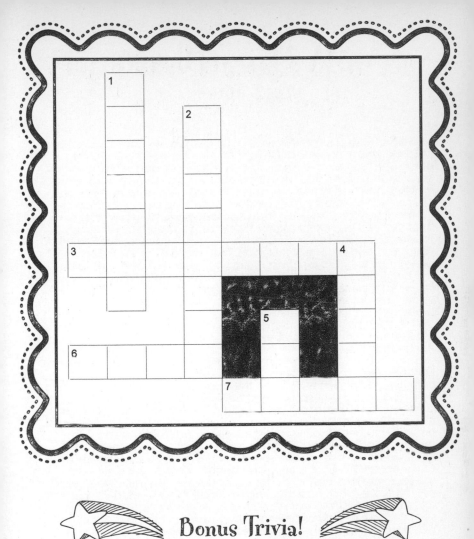

Bonus Trivia!

What strange vision did Ezekiel once have?

    a) a tree in the middle of a tree

    b) a box in the middle of a box

    c) a star in the middle of a star

    d) a wheel in the middle of a wheel

Answer: d) a wheel in the middle of a wheel (Ezekiel 1:16)

19. A Hairy Disaster
JUDGES 16:4–21

And it came to pass afterward, that he loved a woman in the valley of **Sorek**, whose name was Delilah. And the lords of the Philistines came up unto her, and said unto her, Entice him, and see wherein his great strength lieth, and by what means we may prevail against him, that we may bind him to afflict him; and we will give thee every one of us eleven hundred pieces of **silver**. And Delilah said to Samson, Tell me, I pray thee, wherein thy great **strength** lieth, and wherewith thou mightest be bound to afflict thee. And **Samson** said unto her, If they bind me with seven green withs that were never dried, then shall I be weak, and be as another man. Then the lords of the Philistines brought up to her seven green withs which had not been dried, and she bound him with them. Now there were men lying in wait, abiding with her in the chamber. And she said unto him, The Philistines be upon thee, Samson. And he brake the withs, as a thread of tow is broken when it toucheth the fire. So his strength was not known. And Delilah said unto Samson, Behold, thou hast mocked me, and told me lies: now tell me, I pray thee, wherewith thou mightest be bound. And he said unto her, If they bind me fast with new ropes that never were occupied, then shall I be weak, and be as another man. Delilah therefore took **new ropes**, and bound him therewith, and said unto him, The Philistines be upon thee, Samson. And there were liers in wait abiding in the chamber. And he brake them from off his arms like a thread. And **Delilah** said unto Samson, Hitherto thou hast mocked me, and told me lies: tell me wherewith thou mightest be bound. And he said unto her, If thou weavest the seven locks of my head with the web. And she fastened it with the pin, and said unto him, The Philistines be upon thee, Samson. And he awaked out of his sleep, and went away with the pin of the beam, and with the web. And she said unto him, How canst thou say, I love thee, when thine heart is not with me? thou hast mocked me these **three** times, and hast not told me wherein thy great strength lieth. And it came to pass, when she pressed him daily with her words, and urged him, so that his soul was vexed unto death; That he told her all his heart, and said unto her, There hath not come a **razor** upon mine head; for I have been a Nazarite unto God from my mother's womb: if I be shaven, then my strength will go from me, and I shall become **weak**, and be like any other man. And when Delilah saw that he had told her all his heart, she sent and called for the lords of the Philistines, saying, Come up this once, for he hath shewed me all his heart. Then the lords of the Philistines came up unto her, and brought money in their hand. And she made him **sleep** upon her knees; and she called for a man, and she caused him to shave off the seven locks of his head; and she began to afflict him, and his strength went from him. And she said, The Philistines be upon thee, Samson. And he awoke out of his sleep, and said, I will go out as at other times before, and shake myself. And he wist not that the Lord was departed from him. But the Philistines took him, and put out his **eyes**, and brought him down to **Gaza**, and bound him with fetters of brass; and he did grind in the prison house.

```
O K R E V L I S M N
J D I U H B V G Y T
N E W R O P E S H W
F L Y C X D R E T E
S I Z E A N R W G A
G L Q T S O G B N K
N A H Y Z S L E E P
U H Z A J M J R R U
I K R A L A O O T P
T H R E E S W X S D
```

20. Powerful Devotion
RUTH 1:11–17

And ~~Naomi~~ said, Turn again, my **daughters**: why will ye go with me? are there yet any more sons in my womb, that they may be your husbands? Turn again, my daughters, go your way; for I am too ~~old~~ to have an husband. If I should say, I have ~~hope,~~ if I should have an husband also to night, and should also bear sons; would ye tarry for them till they were grown? would ye stay for them from having husbands? nay, my daughters; for it grieveth me much for your sakes that the hand of the LORD is gone out against me. And they lifted up their **voice**, and **wept** again: and Orpah **kissed** her mother in law; but **Ruth** clave unto her. And she said, Behold, thy sister in law is gone back unto her people, and unto her gods: return thou after thy sister in law. And Ruth said, Intreat me not to leave thee, or to return from **following** after thee: for whither thou goest, I will go; and where thou lodgest, I will **lodge**: thy people shall be my **people**, and thy God my **God**: Where thou diest, will I die, and there will I be buried: the LORD do so to me, and more also, if ought but death part thee and me.

T P E W R A W S D G
X D N T U L A L N V
A R A S T S O I G O
Z P O U H S W D F I
M O M B G O D U G C
T Q I N L H O P E E
N S L L O D T F L O
A W O E L P O E P W
L F A C C E B E R E
P K I S S E D I H S

21. Ruth and Boaz
RUTH 3:5-18

And she said unto her, All that thou sayest unto me I will do. And she went down unto the floor, and did according to all that her mother in law bade her. And when **Boaz** had eaten and drunk, and his heart was merry, he went to lie down at the end of the heap of **corn**: and she came softly, and uncovered his **feet**, and laid her down. And it came to pass at midnight, that the man was afraid, and turned himself: and, behold, a woman lay at his feet. And he said, Who art thou? And she answered, I am **Ruth** thine handmaid: spread therefore thy skirt over thine handmaid; for thou art a near **kinsman**. And he said, Blessed be thou of the LORD, my daughter: for thou hast shewed more **kindness** in the latter end than at the beginning, inasmuch as thou followedst not young men, whether poor or rich. And now, my daughter, fear not; I will do to thee all that thou requirest: for all the city of my people doth know that thou art a virtuous woman. And now it is true that I am thy near kinsman: howbeit there is a kinsman nearer than I. Tarry this night, and it shall be in the morning, that if he will perform unto thee the part of a kinsman, well; let him do the kinsman's part: but if he will not do the part of a kinsman to thee, then will I do the part of a kinsman to thee, as the LORD liveth: lie down until the morning. And she lay at his feet until the **morning**: and she rose up before one could know another. And he said, Let it not be known that a woman came into the floor. Also he said, Bring the vail that thou hast upon thee, and hold it. And when she held it, he measured **six** measures of **barley**, and laid it on her: and she went into the city. And when she came to her mother in law, she said, Who art thou, my daughter? And she told her all that the man had done to her. And she said, These six measures of barley gave he me; for he said to me, Go not **empty** unto thy mother in law. Then said she, **Sit** still, my daughter, until thou know how the matter will fall: for the man will not be in rest, until he have **finished** the thing this day.

```
S N A M S N I K X F
T S I X J A K E H I
E R E B E C C A G N
I U A N T O P N G I
L T D Y D R I S Y S
U H M T M N J I T H
J R E U R F I T P E
A E B O A Z M K M D
F S M I B A R L E Y
I L N C A L T X L A
```

22. Hannah's Miracle Baby
1 Samuel 1:1–20

ACROSS

2. One of the things Hannah did in grief (v. 7)

4. Where the priest lived (v. 9)

6. Though Hannah prayed, this was not heard (v. 13)

DOWN

1. What Hannah did after she was promised a baby (v. 18)

2. "The Lord had shut up her _____" (v. 6)

3. Name of Hannah's miracle baby (v. 20)

5. Name of the priest who spoke with Hannah (v. 9)

6. What Hannah made to the Lord (v. 11)

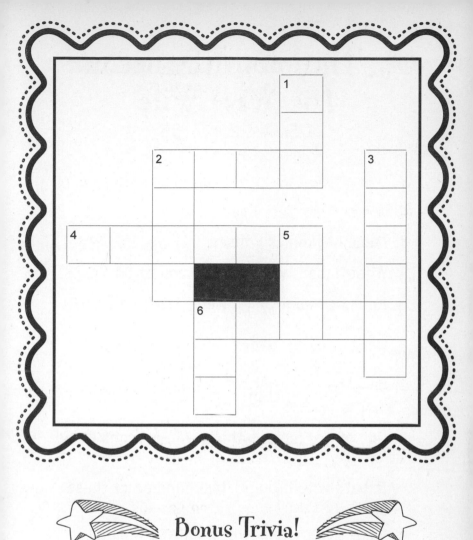

Bonus Trivia!

What kind of tree did Zacchaeus climb in order to see Jesus?

    a) sycamore

    b) oak

    c) palm

    d) crab apple

23. The Foolish Nabal and His Wise Wife

1 Samuel 25:14–35

ACROSS

3. Name of Nabal's wife (v. 14)

7. What Nabal's wife asked David to do (v. 28)

8. Animals Nabal's men were watching (v. 16)

DOWN

1. What David promised to Nabal's wife and her house (v. 35)

2. One of the foods Nabal's wife brought David (v. 18)

4. Nabal's wife brought two hundred of these (v. 18)

5. What Nabal's wife did when she first saw David (v. 23)

6. Number of sheep Nabal's wife brought David (v. 18)

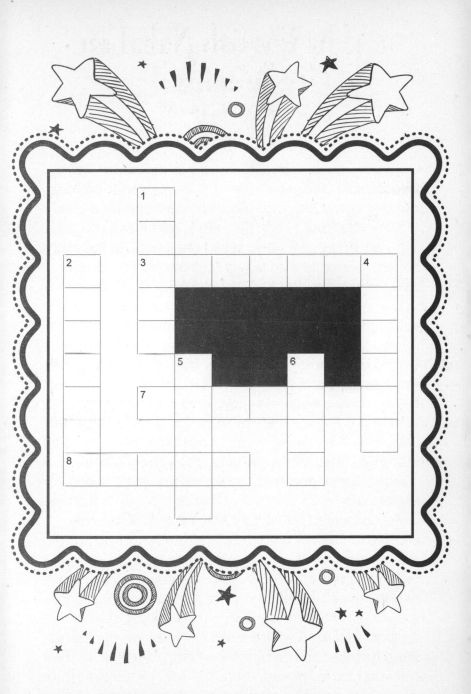

24. A Warning Against Sneering
2 Samuel 6:16–23

And as the ark of the ~~Lord~~ came into the city of David, ~~Michal~~ Saul's daughter looked through a **window**, and saw king David leaping and dancing before the Lord; and she ~~despised~~ him in her heart. And they brought in the ark of the Lord, and set it in his place, in the midst of the tabernacle that ~~David~~ had pitched for it: and David offered burnt **offerings** and peace offerings before the Lord. And as soon as David had made an end of offering burnt offerings and peace offerings, he blessed the people in the name of the Lord of hosts. And he dealt among all the people, even among the whole **multitude** of Israel, as well to the women as men, to every one a cake of bread, and a good piece of flesh, and a flagon of wine. So all the people departed every one to his **house**. Then David returned to bless his household. And Michal the daughter of Saul came out to meet David, and said, How **glorious** was the king of ~~Israel~~ to day, who uncovered himself to day in the eyes of the handmaids of his servants, as one of the vain fellows shamelessly uncovereth himself! And David said unto Michal, It was before the Lord, which chose me before thy ~~father~~, and before all his house, to appoint me ~~ruler~~ over the people of the Lord, over Israel: therefore will I play before the Lord. And I will yet be more vile than thus, and will be base in mine own sight: and of the maidservants which thou hast spoken of, of them shall I be had ~~in~~ **honour**. Therefore Michal the daughter of Saul had no child unto the day of her death.

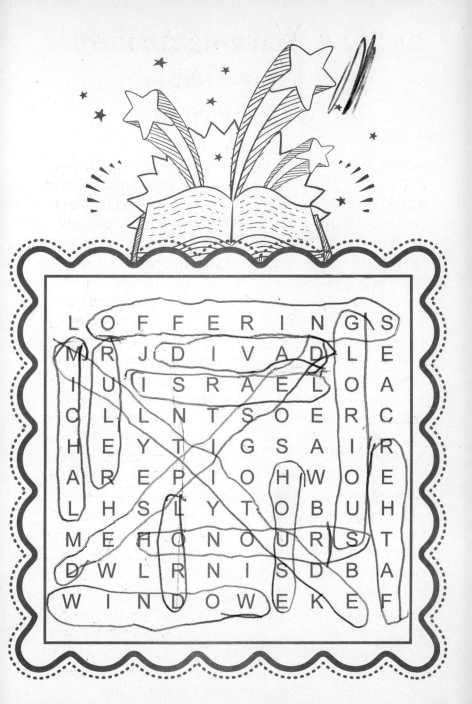

L O F F E R I N G S
M R J D I V A D L E
I U I S R A E L O A
C L L N T S O E R C
H E Y T I G S A I R
A R E P I O H W O E
L H S L Y T O B U H
M E H O N O U R S T
D W L R N I S D B A
W I N D O W E K E F

25. Two Women, Two Babies, and King Solomon's Wise Decision

1 KINGS 3:16–28

ACROSS

2. Child who was taken (v. 20)

3. The "real" relative Solomon had to determine (v. 27)

6. What happened to the other child (v. 19)

7. Time of day the sorry discovery was made (v. 21)

DOWN

1. Day one woman gave birth after her room-mate (v. 18)

2. What the king demanded for making his decision (v. 24)

4. Amount of baby to be given to each woman (v. 25)

5. Which child should be given to the real mother? (v. 27)

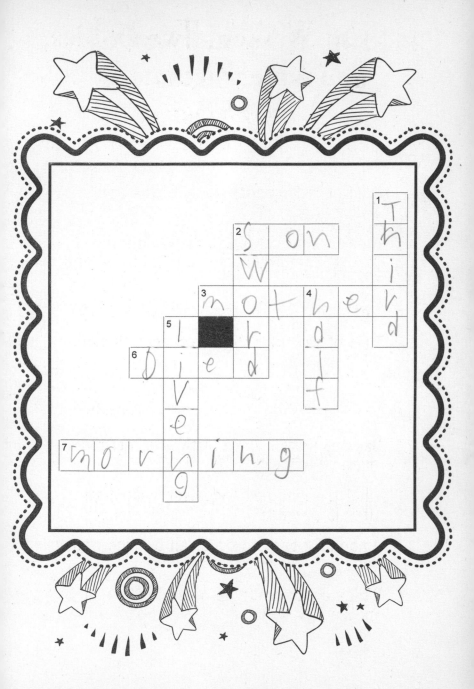

26. A Special Lady Visits Solomon

1 Kings 10:1–13

ACROSS

1. Musical instruments made for the Lord's house (v. 12)

5. Animals that carried the lady's gifts (v. 2)

7. The royal rank the lady had (v. 1)

8. Precious metal the lady brought in large amounts (v. 2)

DOWN

2. One of the gifts the lady brought for Solomon (v. 2)

3. "And Solomon told her all her _____." (v. 3)

4. What the lady heard others tell of Solomon (v. 7)

6. What the lady heard from Solomon (v. 6)

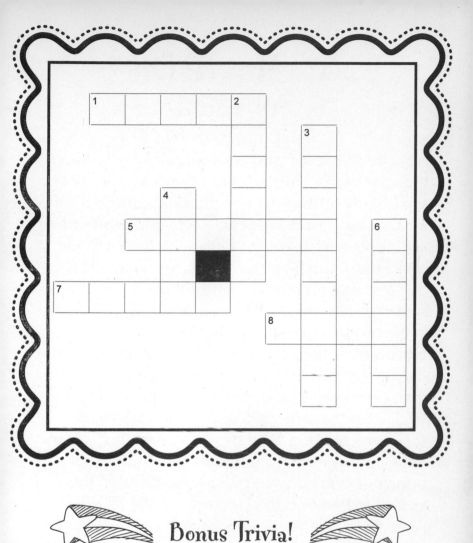

Bonus Trivia!

What is Methuselah famous for?

    a) He was Adam and Eve's favorite movie star.

    b) He was thrown into the fiery furnace.

    c) He was brought back to life by Elijah.

    d) He lived 969 years.

Answer: d) He lived 969 years (Genesis 5:27)

27. Miracle Oil

2 Kings 4:1–7

Now there cried a certain **woman** of the wives of the sons of the prophets unto Elisha, saying, Thy servant my **husband** is dead; and thou knowest that thy servant did fear the Lord: and the **creditor** is come to take unto him my two sons to be bondmen. And **Elisha** said unto her, What shall I do for thee? tell me, what hast thou in the house? And she said, Thine handmaid hath not any thing in the house, save a pot of oil. Then he said, Go, **borrow** thee vessels abroad of all thy neighbours, even empty vessels; borrow not a few. And when thou art come in, thou shalt **shut** the **door** upon thee and upon thy sons, and shalt **pour** out into all those vessels, and thou shalt set aside that which is full. So she went from him, and shut the door upon her and upon her sons, who brought the vessels to her; and she poured out. And it came to pass, when the vessels were **full**, that she said unto her son, Bring me yet a vessel. And he said unto her, There is not a vessel more. And the **oil** stayed. Then she came and told the man of God. And he said, Go, **sell** the oil, and **pay** thy debt, and live thou and thy children of the rest.

```
I O N L P P C L F R
Y U A S J A M L K D
T D M H G B Y E H N
P O O U E L I S H A
D O W T L C V F R B
S R U U E W A Q E S
T C F R F R D X Z U
V G B O R R O W Y H
B C R E D I T O R H
P L M K L O I J N B
```

28. A Boy Brought Back to Life

2 Kings 4:17–36

And the woman conceived, and bare a **son** at that season that Elisha had said unto her, according to the time of life. And when the child was grown, it fell on a day, that he went out to his father to the **reapers**. And he said unto his father, My **head**, my head. And he said to a lad, Carry him to his mother. And when he had taken him, and brought him to his mother, he sat on her knees till noon, and then **died**. And she went up, and laid him on the bed of the man of God, and shut the door upon him, and went out. And she called unto her husband, and said, Send me, I pray thee, one of the young men, and one of the asses, that I may run to the man of God, and come again. And he said, Wherefore wilt thou go to him to day? it is neither new moon, nor sabbath. And she said, It shall be well. Then she saddled an ass, and said to her servant, Drive, and go forward; slack not thy riding for me, except I bid thee. So she went and came unto the man of God to mount **Carmel**. And it came to pass, when the man of God saw her afar off, that he said to **Gehazi** his servant, Behold, yonder is that Shunammite: Run now, I pray thee, to meet her, and say unto her, Is it well with thee? is it well with thy husband? is it well with the child? And she answered, It is well: And when she came to the man of God to the hill, she caught him by the **feet**: but Gehazi came near to thrust her away. And the man of God said, Let her alone; for her soul is vexed within her: and the LORD hath hid it from me, and hath not told me. Then she said, Did I desire a son of my lord? did I not say, Do not deceive me? Then he said to Gehazi, Gird up thy loins, and take my staff in thine hand, and go thy way: if thou meet any man, salute him not; and if any salute thee, answer him not again: and lay my **staff** upon the **face** of the child. And the mother of the child said, As the LORD liveth, and as thy soul liveth, I will not leave thee. And he arose, and followed her. And Gehazi passed on before them, and laid the staff upon the face of the child; but there was neither voice, nor hearing. Wherefore he went again to meet him, and told him, saying, The child is not awaked. And when Elisha was come into the house, behold, the child was dead, and laid upon his bed. He went in therefore, and shut the door upon them twain, and **prayed** unto the LORD. And he went up, and lay upon the child, and put his mouth upon his mouth, and his eyes upon his eyes, and his hands upon his hands: and stretched himself upon the child; and the flesh of the child waxed warm. Then he returned, and walked in the house to and fro; and went up, and **stretched** himself upon him: and the child **sneezed** seven times, and the child opened his eyes. And he called Gehazi, and said, Call this Shunammite. So he called her. And when she was come in unto him, he said, Take up thy son.

D G E H A Z I R L O
E I W K I A Z E F K
H H E A D W M A F M
C S E D U R S P A N
T X D F A Q E E T J
E F A C E Y R R S I
R D E Z E E N S Y U
T Z C L J H T T O H
S A P O M N D F G N
P R A Y E D X C V B

29. If I Perish, I Perish
ESTHER 4:7-17

And Mordecai told him of all that had happened unto him, and of the sum of the money that Haman had promised to pay to the king's treasuries for the **Jews**, to destroy them. Also he gave him the **copy** of the writing of the decree that was given at Shushan to destroy them, to shew it unto Esther, and to declare it unto her, and to charge her that she should go in unto the king, to make supplication unto him, and to make request before him for her people. And Hatach came and told Esther the words of Mordecai. Again Esther spake unto Hatach, and gave him commandment unto Mordecai; All the king's servants, and the people of the king's provinces, do know, that whosoever, whether man or women, shall come unto the king into the inner court, who is not called, there is one law of his to put him to death, except such to whom the king shall hold out the golden sceptre, that he may live: but I have not been called to come in unto the king these thirty days. And they told to Mordecai Esther's words. Then Mordecai commanded to answer Esther, Think not with thyself that thou shalt **escape** in the king's house, more than all the Jews. For if thou altogether holdest thy peace at this time, then shall there enlargement and deliverance arise to the Jews from another place; but thou and thy father's house shall be **destroyed**: and who knoweth whether thou art come to the **kingdom** for such a time as this? Then **Esther** bade them return Mordecai this answer, Go, **gather** together all the Jews that are present in Shushan, and **fast** ye for me, and neither eat nor drink **three** days, night or day: I also and my maidens will fast likewise; and so will I go in unto the **king**, which is not according to the **law**: and if I perish, I **perish**. So Mordecai went his way, and did according to all that Esther had commanded him.

V W B U L C M T F H
G J E W S O B H O K
F A A B D P I R B Y
A L T G O Y L E H S
S R N H M O P E S L
T I A O E A K T I L
K X M S C R M S R O
E D E S T R O Y E D
M R E S T H E R P H
M U S B I L K I N G

30. Esther's Courage Rewarded

ESTHER 7:1–10

So the king and Haman came to banquet with Esther the queen. And the king said again unto Esther on the second day at the banquet of wine, What is thy ⬛⬛, queen Esther? and it shall be granted thee: and what is thy request? and it shall be performed, even to the half of the kingdom. Then **Esther** the queen answered and said, If I have found favour in thy sight, O king, and if it please the king, let my life be given me at my petition, and my people at my request: For we are **sold**, I and my people, to be destroyed, to be **slain**, and to perish. But if we had been sold for bondmen and bondwomen, I had held my tongue, although the enemy could not countervail the king's damage. Then the king Ahasuerus answered and said unto Esther the queen, Who is he, and where is he, that durst presume in his heart to do so? And Esther said, The adversary and enemy is this wicked **Haman**. Then Haman was afraid before the **king** and the **queen**. And the king arising from the banquet of wine in his **wrath** went into the palace garden: and Haman stood up to make request for his life to Esther the queen; for he saw that there was evil determined against him by the king. Then the king returned out of the palace **garden** into the place of the banquet of wine; and Haman was fallen upon the bed whereon Esther was. Then said the king, Will he force the queen also before me in the house? As the word went out of king's mouth, they covered Haman's **face**. And Harbonah, one of the chamberlains, said before the king, Behold also, the gallows fifty cubits high, which Haman had made for Mordecai, who spoken good for the king, standeth in the house of Haman. Then the king said, Hang him thereon. So they hanged Haman on the **gallows** that he had **prepared** for Mordecai. Then was the king's wrath pacified.

```
Y G H G A R D E N E
K L G A L L O W S C
D A I J M P K F D A
E N Y M R A I E N F
R D Q U E E N C O H
A C L F H B G N T S
P B O O T Y T A A L
E P R U S Z R R E A
R M B R E W A F H I
P E T I T I O N W N
```

31. I'm a Sheep!
Psalm 23:1–6

ACROSS

    1. The Lord is this type of person (v. 1)

    3. Sometimes we walk through this (v. 4)

    5. Another name for God (v. 1)

    7. What God makes us do in green pastures (v. 2)

    8. It's poured out to "anoint" us (v. 5)

    9. Where God leads us in righteousness (v. 3)

DOWN

    1. The hint of death (v. 4)

    2. The part of the body that's anointed (v. 5)

    4. God prepares a table in whose presence? (v. 5)

    6. Time measure of goodness and mercy (v. 6)

32. One Amazing Woman
PROVERBS 31:29–31

Many daughters have done **virtuously**, but thou excellest them all. **Favour** is **deceitful**, and **beauty** is **vain**: but a **woman** that feareth the LORD, she shall be **praised**. Give her of the **fruit** of her **hands**; and let her own works praise her in the **gates**.

A	W	X	D	B	H	A	N	D	S
L	U	F	T	I	E	C	E	D	R
O	F	V	A	N	G	A	T	E	S
R	R	D	J	V	I	L	U	P	Q
D	U	E	Z	S	O	E	C	T	F
N	I	S	T	B	N	U	H	U	Y
I	T	I	M	K	A	O	R	E	D
A	C	A	T	G	M	A	N	Y	B
V	I	R	T	U	O	U	S	L	Y
U	J	P	M	O	W	L	W	S	X

Bonus Trivia!

What did God give Daniel the ability to explain?
- a) other languages
- b) smoke signals
- c) dreams
- d) the words in rap songs

Answer: c) dreams (Daniel 2:1-19)

33. Hungry Beasts, Brave Young Man

DANIEL 6:4–28

ACROSS

2. How many days did the king's foolish law last? (v. 7)

4. Another term for the king's law (v. 12)

5. Name of man thrown into the den (v. 16)

8. Object used to cover the mouth of the den (v. 17)

DOWN

1. What the young man did, as he had every day (v. 10)

3. Number of times per day the young man gave thanks to God (v. 10)

4. Name of the king (v. 9)

6. Whom God sent to shut all the beasts' mouths (v. 22)

7. Animals kept in the den (v. 16)

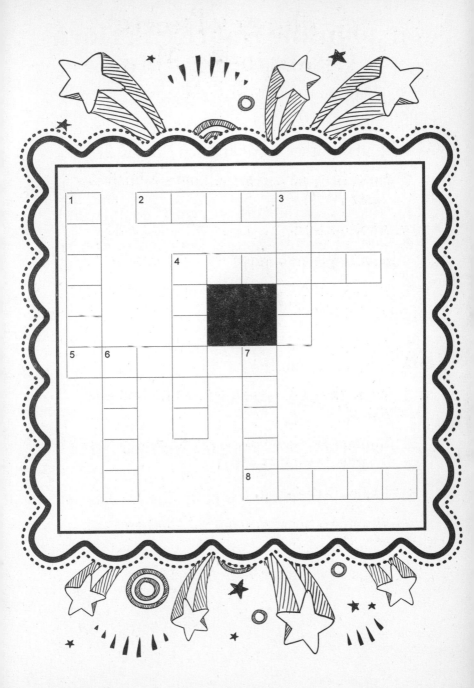

34. John the Baptist Is Born
Luke 1:57-66

ACROSS

   3. John's mother brought forth this (v. 57)

   5. Name of John's mother (v. 57)

   7. "The ___ of the Lord was with" John (v. 66)

   8. Relative people thought the baby should be named after (v. 59)

DOWN

   1. How the father—who couldn't speak—communicated the baby's name (v. 63)

   2. "And his _____ was opened immediately." (v. 64)

   4. How people communicated with the father (v. 62)

   6. Number of the day the baby was circumcised (v. 59)

35. Mary Is Chosen
Luke 1:26–38

And in the **sixth** month the angel **Gabriel** was sent from **God** unto a city of Galilee, named Nazareth, to a **virgin** espoused to a man whose name was Joseph, of the house of David; and the virgin's name was Mary. And the angel came in unto her, and said, Hail, thou that art highly favoured, the Lord is with thee: **blessed** art thou among women. And when she saw him, she was **troubled** at his saying, and cast in her mind what manner of salutation this should be. And the angel said unto her, Fear not, Mary: for thou hast found favour with God. And, behold, thou shalt conceive in thy womb, and bring forth a **son**, and shalt call his name Jesus. He shall be great, and shall be called the Son of the Highest: and the Lord God shall give unto him the throne of his father David: And he shall reign over the house of Jacob for ever; and of his kingdom there shall be no end. Then said **Mary** unto the angel, How shall this be, seeing I know not a man? And the angel answered and said unto her, The Holy Ghost shall come upon thee, and the power of the Highest shall **overshadow** thee: therefore also that holy thing which shall be born of thee shall be called the Son of God. And, behold, thy cousin Elisabeth, she hath also conceived a son in her **old** age: and this is the sixth month with her, who was called barren. For with God **nothing** shall be impossible. And Mary said, Behold the handmaid of the Lord; be it unto me according to thy word. And the angel departed from her.

```
O V E R S H A D O W
S V P O I U T Y R E
W I Q G A B R I E L
G R X L K A J H E S
N G G T M F D G U S
I I A M H N A S B V
H N X Z E D E C G B
T H Y N L J U M O K
O T R O U B L E D I
N D E S S E L B L O
```

36. Baby Jesus' First Visitors

Luke 2:8–14

ACROSS

2. What the glory of the Lord did around these people (v. 9)

3. First thing announced for those on earth (v. 14)

6. How Christ the Lord came to earth (v. 11)

7. What came with the good tidings? (two words, v. 10)

DOWN

1. Who appeared to baby Jesus' first visitors? (v. 9)

2. What was the visitors' job? (v. 8)

4. Word of praise spoken to God (v. 14)

5. What was Baby Jesus lying in? (v. 12)

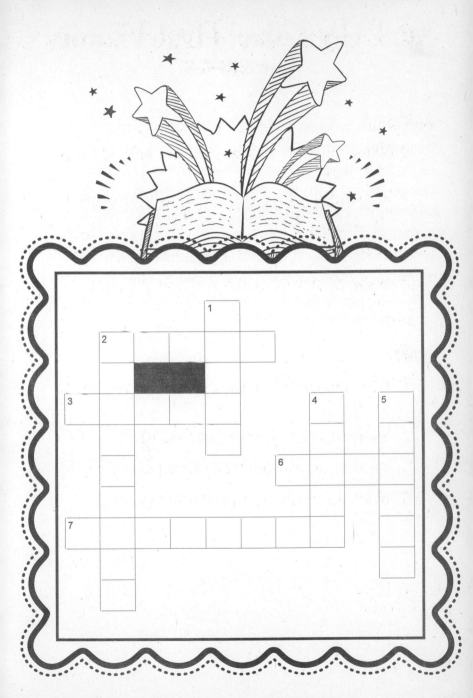

37. Anna Meets Baby Jesus
LUKE 2:36–38

And there was one **Anna**, a **prophetess**, the **daughter** of Phanuel, of the tribe of Aser: she was of a great **age**, and had lived with an husband **seven** years from her virginity; and she was a **widow** of about fourscore and four years, which departed not from the temple, but **served** God with fastings and prayers night and **day**. And she coming in that **instant** gave **thanks** likewise unto the Lord, and **spake** of him to all them that **looked** for redemption in Jerusalem.

```
O K M N J Y I U H S
T B S P A K E V S R
N W I D O W G E E E
A H D U S Y T F R T
T C E X D E G A V H
S R K A H E V S E G
N Z O P N A W E D U
I Q O P L N I K N A
M R L J U Y A H N D
P B G R T H A N K S
```

Bonus Trivia!

What did the people of Babel try to build to reach the heavens?

    a) a rocket

    b) a ladder

    c) a staircase

    d) a tower

Answer: d) a tower (Genesis 11:1–9)

38. More Visitors for Young Jesus
MATTHEW 2:1–12

Now when **Jesus** was born in Bethlehem of Judaea in the days of Herod the king, behold, there came wise men from the east to Jerusalem, saying, Where is he that is **born** King of the Jews? for we have seen his **star** in the east, and are come to worship him. When Herod the king had heard these things, he was troubled, and all Jerusalem with him. And when he had gathered all the chief priests and scribes of the people together, he demanded of them where Christ should be born. And they said unto him, In **Bethlehem** of Judaea: for thus it is written by the prophet, And thou Bethlehem, in the land of Juda, art not the least among the princes of Juda: for out of thee shall come a Governor, that shall rule my people Israel. Then Herod, when he had privily called the wise men, enquired of them diligently what time the star appeared. And he sent them to Bethlehem, and said, Go and search diligently for the young child; and when ye have found him, bring me word again, that I may come and **worship** him also. When they had heard the **king**, they departed; and, lo, the star, which they saw in the **east**, went before them, till it came and stood over where the young child was. When they saw the star, they rejoiced with exceeding great joy. And when they were come into the house, they saw the young **child** with Mary his mother, and fell down, and worshipped him: and when they had opened their treasures, they presented unto him **gifts**; **gold**, and frankincense and **myrrh**. And being warned of God in a **dream** that they should not return to Herod, they departed into their own country another way.

```
B J A D I V K I N G
O E C P K S A N F I
R S T I D L I H C F
N U X H T S E R F T
W S U S L I W C H S
S H A R E E B R R Q
A E G O L D H Q R I
R D A W U H Y E Y C
L O V E D R E A M N
S T A R H O X I P V
```

39. Jesus' First Miracle
JOHN 2:1–10

ACROSS

2. The ruler of the feast did this to a special drink (v. 9)

5. Jesus miraculously made this (v. 9)

6. Town where the wedding party took place (v. 1)

7. Large pots were made out of this material (v. 6)

DOWN

1. What liquid did Jesus start with? (v. 9)

3. Jesus' command after the miracle (v. 8)

4. Name of the region where the miracle occurred (v. 1)

7. Number of large pots (v. 6)

Bonus Trivia!

What did the Holy Spirit look like when it came down on Jesus after His baptism?

a) a dove

b) a cloud

c) a hawk

d) lightning

Answer: a) a dove (Luke 3:21-22)

40. Dinner with Sinners
MATTHEW 9:9–13

And as Jesus passed forth from thence, he saw a man, named **Matthew**, **sitting** at the receipt of custom: and he saith unto him, **<u>Follow me</u>**. And he arose, and followed him. And it came to pass, as Jesus sat at meat in the **house**, behold, many publicans and sinners came and sat down with him and his disciples. And when the Pharisees saw it, they said unto his disciples, Why eateth your Master with publicans and **sinners**? But when **Jesus** heard that, he said unto them, They that be whole need not a physician, but they that are **sick**. But go ye and learn what that meaneth, I will have mercy, and not **sacrifice**: for I am not come to call the **righteous**, but sinners to repentance.

```
E M W O L L O F R S
S W S I N N E R S U
T A I J E S U S M O
F Y C V M O M S A E
D G K R S A R A T T
U O L M I S A S T H
V S R U O F R S H G
E S U O H X I W E I
B K J H G F D C W R
A S I T T I N G E S
```

Bonus Trivia!

What did Jesus say a wise man builds his house on?

    a) a gold mine
    b) sand
    c) rock
    d) a riverbank

Answer: c) rock (Luke 6:47–48)

41. The Healing Touch
LUKE 8:43–48

And a woman having an issue of blood **twelve** years, which had spent all her living upon **physicians**, neither could be healed of any, came behind him, and **touched** the **border** of his garment: and immediately her issue of **blood** stanched. And Jesus said, Who touched me? When all denied, **Peter** and they that were with him said, Master, the multitude throng thee and **press** thee, and sayest thou, Who touched me? And Jesus said, Somebody hath touched me: for I perceive that virtue is gone out of me. And when the **woman** saw that she was not hid, she came **trembling**, and falling down before him, she declared unto him before all the people for what cause she had touched him, and how she was **healed** immediately. And he said unto her, Daughter, be of good comfort: thy **faith** hath made thee whole; go in **peace**.

```
P R E S S Q W E R T
Y H U I O P A S E D
F G Y H E A L E D H
J K L S Z X C E R B
E P F A I T H W O L
V E E V B C N O B O
L A M T U U I M H O
E C B O E V W A Z D
W E T R D R X N N A
T R E M B L I N G S
```

42. Jesus Raises a Church Leader's Daughter

MATTHEW 9:23–26

And when **Jesus** came into the ruler's **house**, and saw the minstrels and the **people** making a **noise**, he said unto them, Give place: for the maid is not dead, but sleepeth. And they **laughed** him to **scorn**. But when the people were put forth, he went in, and **took** her by the **hand**, and the maid **arose**. And the **fame** hereof went **abroad** into all that **land**.

```
E  D  C  V  F  N  R  K  T  G
B  N  H  D  P  E  O  P  L  E
F  Y  N  U  J  O  M  I  E  K
I  A  O  L  T  E  P  S  S  J
L  W  M  A  Q  S  U  Z  S  E
E  R  D  E  X  O  C  D  F  S
T  Y  G  V  H  R  N  B  H  U
S  C  O  R  N  A  U  I  J  S
N  M  D  E  H  G  U  A  L  K
O  A  B  R  O  A  D  P  A  N
```

Bonus Trivia!

Who gave the five loaves and two fish that Jesus used to feed five thousand people?

    a) Long John Silver

    b) Peter

    c) Jesus' mother, Mary

    d) a little boy

Answer: d) a little boy (John 6:9)

43. Walking on Water
MATTHEW 14:22–33

And straightway Jesus constrained his disciples to get into a ship, and to go before him unto the other side, while he sent the multitudes away. And when he had sent the multitudes away, he went up into a mountain apart to **pray**: and when the evening was come, he was there alone. But the ship was now in the midst of the sea, tossed with waves: for the **wind** was contrary. And in the **fourth** watch of the night Jesus went unto them, **walking** on the sea. And when the disciples saw him walking on the sea, they were troubled, saying, It is a spirit; and they cried out for **fear**. But straightway Jesus spake unto them, saying, Be of good cheer; it is I; be not afraid. And **Peter** answered him and said, **Lord**, if it be thou, bid me come unto thee on the water. And he said, **Come**. And when Peter was come down out of the ship, he walked on the water, to go to Jesus. But when he saw the wind boisterous, he was afraid; and beginning to **sink**, he cried, saying, Lord, <u>**save me**</u>. And immediately Jesus stretched forth his **hand**, and caught him, and said unto him, O thou of little faith, wherefore didst thou **doubt**? And when they were come into the ship, the wind ceased. Then they that were in the ship came and worshipped him, saying, Of a truth thou art the Son of God.

```
R S E V B H O U C O
W A Y H A N S T O E
O P E T E R E P M T
W R Q F H I D E E P
I A H C A T V J N H
N Y L L E A R U O A
D P I K S T R U G N
R W A L I T B U O D
A C F E N N I C E F
L O R D K A G T U K
```

44. Jesus Heals Simon's Mother-In-Law

MARK 1:29–31

And forthwith, when they were **come** out of the **synagogue**, they entered into the house of **Simon** and **Andrew**, with James and John. But Simon's wife's **mother** lay **sick** of a **fever**, and anon they tell him of her. And he came and **took** her by the **hand**, and **lifted** her up; and immediately the fever **left** her, and she **ministered** unto them.

```
D S I M O N A S F G
H Y J K L R Z X C K
V N B N E M Q W C E
R A T H A N D I Y W
U G T I L O S K P E
E O E L D I C O V R
M G R E V E F O F D
O U R F T G B T N N
C E H T Y U J M E A
M I N I S T E R E D
```

Bonus Trivia!

What did Satan tell Jesus to turn into bread?

    a) a turtle
    b) His sandal
    c) a scroll
    d) stones

45. Friends Help a Man Find Healing

Mark 2:1–12

ACROSS

2. What Jesus saw in the men (v. 5)

3. City the miracle occurred in (v. 1)

6. What the friends broke through (v. 4)

8. The crowd blocked this (v. 2)

DOWN

1. One word in Jesus' conversation with the scribes (v. 9)

4. People's reaction when the paralyzed man walked (v. 12)

5. Why the men cut through the ceiling (two words, v. 2)

7. Number of people who carried the paralyzed man (v. 3)

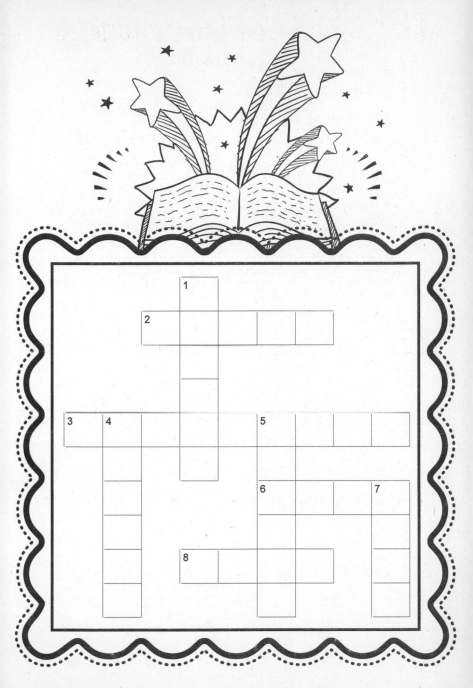

97

46. The Four Soils
MARK 4:1–20

ACROSS

2. How fruit appeared on the good ground (two words, v. 8)

3. What a farmer does with seed (v. 3)

5. The plants that choked everything (v. 7)

7. What does the seed in this parable represent? (v. 14)

DOWN

1. What Jesus did with His parables (v. 2)

2. The sun did this to the plants (v. 6)

4. What the bad plants did to the new plants (v. 7)

6. One possible amount of return for each seed (v. 8)

47. Mountaintop Transfiguration

MARK 9:2–10

And after **six days** Jesus taketh with him Peter, and **James**, and **John**, and leadeth them up into an high mountain apart by themselves: and he was transfigured before them. And his raiment became shining, exceeding white as snow; so as no fuller on earth can white them. And there appeared unto them Elias with Moses: and they were **talking** with Jesus. And **Peter** answered and said to Jesus, Master, it is good for us to be here: and let us make three tabernacles; one for thee, and one for **Moses**, and one for Elias. For he wist not what to say; for they were sore afraid. And there was a **cloud** that overshadowed them: and a voice came out of the cloud, saying, This is my beloved Son: hear him. And suddenly, when they had looked round about, they saw no man any more, save Jesus only with themselves. And as they came down from the **mountain**, he charged them that they should tell no man what things they had seen, till the Son of man were **risen** from the dead. And they kept that saying with themselves, questioning one with another what the rising from the dead should mean.

A	S	D	F	P	O	I	U	Y	D
H	J	A	M	E	S	E	M	A	U
A	O	N	X	T	C	S	N	U	O
P	H	E	S	E	B	I	N	A	L
O	N	E	T	R	A	X	O	L	C
S	U	L	D	T	A	D	Z	V	L
E	S	I	N	Q	U	A	D	U	O
S	T	U	C	B	F	Y	H	K	U
O	O	Y	P	R	I	S	E	N	P
M	A	T	A	L	K	I	N	G	I

48. Children and the Kingdom of God
MARK 10:13–16

And they brought young **children** to him, that he should **touch** them: and his **disciples rebuked** those that brought them. But when **Jesus** saw it, he was much displeased, and said unto them, Suffer the **little** children to **come** unto me, and forbid them not: for of such is the kingdom of **God**. Verily I say unto you, Whosoever shall not receive the **kingdom** of God as a little **child**, he shall not enter therein. And he took them up in his **arms**, put his hands upon them, and **blessed** them.

C	D	E	K	U	B	E	R	E	T
A	U	V	C	K	L	Z	J	O	Y
C	O	M	E	T	O	U	C	H	A
H	B	I	T	O	D	U	D	R	T
W	K	I	N	G	D	O	M	C	K
D	L	U	J	K	I	S	G	J	O
E	A	T	B	L	E	S	S	E	D
C	H	I	L	D	R	E	N	S	N
D	L	I	H	C	H	I	L	U	Y
D	I	S	C	I	P	L	E	S	A

Bonus Trivia!

What were Egypt's kings called?

- a) satraps
- b) proconsuls
- c) pharaohs
- d) scary

49. A Poor Woman's Rich Gift

MARK 12:41–44

And **Jesus** sat over against the **treasury**, and beheld how the people cast **money** into the treasury: and many that were **rich** cast in **much**. And there came a certain poor **widow**, and she threw in **two** mites, which make a farthing. And he called unto him his disciples, and saith unto them, Verily I say unto you, That this **poor** widow hath cast **more** in, than all they which have cast into the treasury: For all they did cast in of their **abundance**; but she of her want did cast in all that she had, even **all** her **living**.

```
V C T D M U C H E W
W N B R G T M C R F
R I C H E U N O Y H
O M D Q I A K M R J
O R O O D O S E W E
P O I N W W U U Y T
B V U C E T X Z R P
A B C M N Y A L L Y
A J E S U S G F D S
L K L I V I N G J H
```

Bonus Trivia!

What kind of bush did God use to get Moses' attention?

- a) flowering
- b) singing
- c) burning
- d) walking

Answer: c) burning (Exodus 3:2–3)

50. The Good Neighbor
Luke 10:30–37

And Jesus answering said, A certain man went down from **Jerusalem** to **Jericho**, and fell among thieves, which stripped him of his raiment, and wounded him, and departed, leaving him **half dead**. And by chance there came down a certain **priest** that way: and when he saw him, he passed by on the **other** side. And likewise a **Levite**, when he was at the place, came and looked on him, and passed by on the other side. But a certain **Samaritan**, as he journeyed, came where he was: and when he saw him, he had compassion on him, and went to him, and bound up his **wounds**, pouring in **oil** and **wine**, and set him on his own beast, and brought him to an **inn**, and took care of him. And on the morrow when he departed, he took out two pence, and gave them to the host, and said unto him, Take care of him; and whatsoever thou spendest more, when I come again, I will repay thee. Which now of these three, thinkest thou, was neighbour unto him that fell among the thieves? And he said, He that shewed **mercy** on him. Then said Jesus unto him, Go, and do thou likewise.

```
D S H A R P S O K C
S A M A R I T A N R
J R E E L D A W B N
E M L T K F O I L W
R T A I L T D N C O
I V S V H A N E P U
C O U E E N I C A N
H V R L I W A S Q D
O H E M E R C Y S S
T A J S T O P U D L
```

51. Disabled Lady Healed on the Sabbath!

Luke 13:10–17

And he was **teaching** in one of the **synagogues** on the sabbath. And, behold, there was a woman which had a spirit of **infirmity** eighteen years, and was bowed together, and could in no wise lift up herself. And when Jesus saw her, he called her to him, and said unto her, Woman, thou art loosed from thine infirmity. And he laid his **hands** on her: and immediately she was made straight, and glorified God. And the ruler of the synagogue answered with indignation, because that Jesus had **healed** on the **sabbath** day, and said unto the people, There are **six** days in which men ought to work: in them therefore come and be healed, and not on the sabbath day. The Lord then answered him, and said, Thou **hypocrite**, doth not each one of you on the sabbath loose his ox or his ass from the stall, and lead him away to watering? And ought not this **woman**, being a daughter of Abraham, whom **Satan** hath bound, lo, these **eighteen** years, be loosed from this bond on the sabbath day? And when he had said these things, all his adversaries were ashamed: and all the people **rejoiced** for all the glorious things that were done by him.

```
H E A L E D W S X S
C N T D E R F G V A
B A S I S D N A H B
Y T I M R I F N I B
G A X T H C Y H N A
M S J C U I O K L T
O N A M O W P P R H
S E U G O G A N Y S
T R E J O I C E D H
M E I G H T E E N S
```

52. A Prodigal ("Wasteful") Man

LUKE 15:11–24

ACROSS

3. The father had this toward his prodigal son (v. 20)

4. The second thing the father gave his returning son (v. 22)

6. The first thing the father gave his returning son (v. 22)

7. The returning son asked to be this type of servant (v. 19)

8. The father's servants had enough bread and this much more (with "to," v. 17)

DOWN

1. Which of the two sons was prodigal? (v. 12)

2. Whom did the prodigal son join with in a far country? (v. 15)

5. Where did the prodigal son feed pigs? (v. 15)

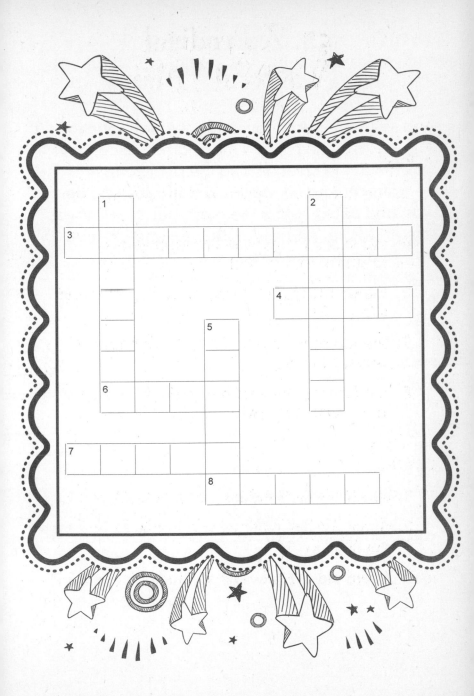

53. Zacchaeus
LUKE 19:1–10

And Jesus entered and passed through **Jericho**. And, behold, there was a man named **Zacchaeus**, which was the chief among the publicans, and he was rich. And he sought to see Jesus who he was; and could not for the press, because he was little of stature. And he ran before, and **climbed** up into a **sycomore** tree to see him: for he was to pass that way. And when Jesus came to the place, he looked **up**, and saw him, and said unto him, Zacchaeus, make haste, and come **down**; for to day I must abide at thy house. And he made haste, and came down, and received him joyfully. And when they saw it, they all murmured, saying, That he was gone to be guest with a man that is a **sinner**. And Zacchaeus stood, and said unto the Lord: Behold, Lord, the half of my goods I give to the **poor**; and if I have taken any thing from any man by false accusation, I restore him fourfold. And Jesus said unto him, This day is salvation come to this house, forsomuch as he also is a son of Abraham. For the Son of man is come to **seek** and to **save** that which was **lost**.

```
S Y C O M O R E L P
K H G R A T S O F A
I E P T E A H S O R
S U E A H C C A Z P
I K E S I D L V D K
N E C R V E I E S A
N W E O L T M F Y O
E J O B J S B A U Y
R D I N W O E W P T
A B P V U L D O W N
```

54. Born Twice
John 3:1–8

There was a man of the **Pharisees**, named **Nicodemus**, a ruler of the Jews: The same came to Jesus by **night**, and said unto him, **Rabbi**, we know that thou art a teacher come from God: for no man can do these miracles that thou doest, except God be with him. Jesus answered and said unto him, Verily, verily, I say unto thee, Except a man be **born again**, he cannot see the kingdom of God. Nicodemus saith unto him, How can a man be born when he is **old**? can he enter the **second** time into his **mother's** womb, and be born? Jesus answered, Verily, verily, I say unto thee, Except a man be born of **water** and of the **Spirit**, he cannot enter into the kingdom of **God**. That which is born of the **flesh** is flesh; and that which is born of the Spirit is spirit. Marvel not that I said unto thee, Ye must be born again. The wind bloweth where it listeth, and thou hearest the sound thereof, but canst not tell whence it cometh, and whither it goeth: so is every one that is born of the Spirit.

```
A  K  M  S  P  I  R  I  T  N
N  I  G  H  T  T  F  O  N  I
S  I  I  R  V  E  Z  Y  R  C
P  H  A  R  I  S  E  E  S  O
C  D  U  G  D  T  A  H  Q  D
W  N  F  R  A  B  B  I  U  E
A  O  L  D  W  N  N  B  M  M
T  C  E  R  A  S  R  G  O  U
E  E  S  R  E  H  T  O  M  S
R  S  H  S  A  R  A  D  B  M
```

55. Feeding the 5,000
John 6:5–14

When Jesus then lifted up his eyes, and saw a great company come unto him, he saith unto **Philip**, Whence shall we buy **bread**, that these may eat? And this he said to prove him: for he himself knew what he would do. Philip answered him, Two hundred pennyworth of bread is not sufficient for them, that every one of them may take a little. One of his disciples, **Andrew**, Simon Peter's brother, saith unto him, There is a lad here, which hath **five** barley loaves, and **two** small fishes: but what are they among **so many**? And Jesus said, Make the men **sit** down. Now there was much grass in the place. So the men sat down, in number about five thousand. And Jesus took the loaves; and when he had given **thanks**, he distributed to the disciples, and the disciples to them that were set down; and likewise of the fishes as much as they would. When they were filled, he said unto his disciples, **Gather** up the fragments that remain, that nothing be lost. Therefore they gathered them together, and filled **twelve baskets** with the fragments of the five **barley** loaves, which remained over and above unto them that had eaten. Then those men, when they had seen the miracle that Jesus did, said, This is of a truth that prophet that should come into the world.

```
A  P  H  I  L  I  P  S  A  E
R  I  C  B  U  Y  T  W  O  N
F  D  E  D  A  E  W  H  P  U
R  A  S  T  K  R  E  V  E  T
E  E  A  S  Y  E  L  O  T  H
H  R  A  O  F  I  V  E  E  A
T  B  Q  M  W  M  E  C  Y  N
A  X  I  A  N  D  R  E  W  K
G  N  U  N  I  S  I  T  P  S
F  U  I  Y  T  H  E  A  R  O
```

56. A Blind Man Sees
John 9:1–11

And as Jesus passed by, he saw a man which was **blind** from his **birth**. And his disciples asked him, saying, Master, who did sin, this man, or his parents, that he was born blind? Jesus answered, Neither hath this man sinned, nor his parents: but that the works of God should be made manifest in him. I must work the works of him that sent me, while it is day: the night cometh, when no man can work. As long as I am in the world, I am the light of the world. When he had thus spoken, he spat on the **ground**, and made clay of the spittle, and he anointed the **eyes** of the blind man with the clay, And said unto him, Go, **wash** in the **pool** of **Siloam**, (which is by interpretation, **Sent**.) He went his way therefore, and washed, and came **seeing**. The neighbours therefore, and they which before had seen him that he was blind, said, Is not this he that sat and begged? Some said, This is he: others said, He is like him: but he said, I am he. Therefore said they unto him, How were thine eyes **opened**? He answered and said, A man that is called Jesus made clay, and anointed mine eyes, and said unto me, Go to the pool of Siloam, and wash: and I went and washed, and I received sight.

```
A N D O H T R I B U
C T N P G A W N M R
D S I L O A M P Y T
I E L A S P I Z Z A
L E B H I Y E Y E S
G I T M B A P N O N
J N U L T C V M E P
Q G R O U N D G S D
X I O O C I E B A T
E A Z P G F H S S Q
```

57. A Widow's Dead Son
Luke 7:11–17

And it came to pass the day after, that he went into a city called **Nain**; and many of his disciples went with him, and much people. Now when he came nigh to the **gate** of the city, behold, there was a **dead** man carried out, the only **son** of his **mother**, and she was a **widow**: and much people of the city was with her. And when the Lord saw her, he had **compassion** on her, and said unto her, Weep not. And he came and **touched** the bier: and they that bare him <u>**stood still**</u>. And he said, **Young** man, I say unto thee, **Arise**. And he that was dead **sat** up, and began to speak. And he delivered him to his mother. And there came a fear on all: and they glorified God, saying, That a great prophet is risen up among us; and, That God hath visited his people. And this rumour of him went forth throughout all Judaea, and throughout all the region round about.

```
S F H W I Q G A T N
A T N I A N A R O R
T S O D U Z N I U G
Y O J O P A S S C B
H U Y W D S O E H H
N T L Y A S N I E U
M E B P E F T O D E
J Q M R D H E I T I
M O T H E R R A L A
C U X W L K G P R L
```

Bonus Trivia!

What color rope did Rahab put in her window to protect herself and her family?

- a) scarlet
- b) purple
- c) green
- d) periwinkle

58. Jesus Anointed
Luke 7:36–50

ACROSS

1. What the person did to Jesus' feet (v. 44)

2. What one man owed, in Jesus' parable (v. 41)

5. Kind of box the person brought to Jesus (v. 37)

6. Number of debtors in Jesus' parable (v. 41)

DOWN

1. The person who washed and wiped Jesus' feet (v. 44)

3. What the woman kissed, over and over (v. 45)

4. What saved the woman (v. 50)

7. What Simon did not pour on Jesus' head (v. 46)

59. Squabbling Sister
LUKE 10:38–42

Now it came to pass, as they went, that he entered into a certain village: and a certain woman named **Martha** received him into her house. And she had a **sister** called **Mary**, which also sat at Jesus' **feet**, and heard his word. But Martha was cumbered about much **serving**, and came to him, and said, Lord, dost thou not care that my sister hath left me to serve **alone**? bid her therefore that she **help** me. And Jesus **answered** and said unto her, Martha, Martha, thou art **careful** and troubled about many things: But one thing is **needful**: and Mary hath **chosen** that **good** part, which shall not be taken away from her.

```
S  X  L  U  F  D  E  E  N  D
C  M  A  R  T  H  A  D  O  E
R  A  F  V  B  G  T  O  Y  D
C  R  H  N  G  E  G  M  J  E
A  Y  H  U  N  F  E  E  T  R
R  I  E  O  I  K  L  O  E  E
E  P  L  Q  V  A  Z  T  X  W
F  A  P  F  R  T  S  Y  G  S
U  V  B  H  E  I  U  I  J  N
L  C  H  O  S  E  N  O  K  A
```

Bonus Trivia!

What were Peter and Andrew doing when Jesus asked them to be His disciples?

- a) playing chess
- b) building a house
- c) fishing
- d) cooking dinner

Answer: c) fishing (Matthew 4:18–19)

60. A Woman's Lost Coin
LUKE 15:8–10

Either what **woman** having **ten** pieces of **silver**, if she **lose** one piece, doth not **light** a **candle**, and **sweep** the house, and **seek** diligently till she **find** it? And when she hath found it, she calleth her **friends** and her neighbours together, saying, Rejoice with me; for I have found the piece which I had lost. Likewise, I say unto you, there is joy in the presence of the **angels** of God over one sinner that **repenteth**.

```
I  S  I  L  V  E  R  O  S  K
S  W  R  D  S  E  W  N  D  A
Y  E  G  V  L  C  E  F  N  T
H  E  E  D  K  T  L  O  E  P
J  P  N  K  U  H  I  D  I  N
B  A  T  R  N  G  N  M  R  A
C  W  E  D  C  I  V  F  F  M
A  Z  X  S  F  L  O  S  E  O
T  A  N  G  E  L  S  W  O  W
R  E  P  E  N  T  E  T  H  Q
```

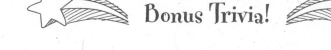

Bonus Trivia!

How were Cain and Abel related?

    a) father and son
    b) brothers
    c) cousins
    d) just third-grade classmates

Answer: b) brothers (Genesis 4:1–2)

61. The Widow and the Judge
LUKE 18:1–8

And he spake a **parable** unto them to this end, that men ought always to **pray**, and not to faint; saying, There was in a city a **judge**, which feared not God, neither regarded man: And there was a **widow** in that city; and she came unto him, saying, Avenge me of mine **adversary**. And he would not for a while: but afterward he said within himself, Though I fear not God, nor regard man; yet because this widow troubleth me, I will **avenge** her, lest by her continual **coming** she weary me. And the Lord said, Hear what the **unjust** judge saith. And shall not God avenge his own elect, which **cry** day and **night** unto him, though he bear long with them? I tell you that he will avenge them speedily. Nevertheless when the Son of man cometh, shall he **find** faith on the **earth**?

```
F W E R U N J U S T
T I Y J U W I A O H
P A N U O S D D E G
F G H D E J K V G I
G L I G L Z X E N N
N W C E B V H R E B
I N M K A T O S V P
M L J I R C U A A H
O B V A A G R R Y T
C R E D P R A Y S E
```

Bonus Trivia!

What did God tell Abraham to do to his son Isaac?
- a) make him eat spinach
- b) give him to the priest
- c) teach him to play the harp
- d) sacrifice him

Answer: d) sacrifice him (Genesis 22:2)

62. Parable of Girls and a Wedding

Matthew 25:1–13

ACROSS

3. Whom were the girls going to meet? (v. 1)

4. Liquid that five girls failed to take (v. 3)

6. Time of day a cry went out (v. 6)

8. Total number of girls in the parable (v. 1)

DOWN

1. How Jesus described the girls who were prepared (v. 8)

2. How Jesus described the girls who were not prepared (v. 3)

5. Objects all of the girls carried (v. 7)

7. What the unprepared girls wanted the prepared girls to do (v. 8)

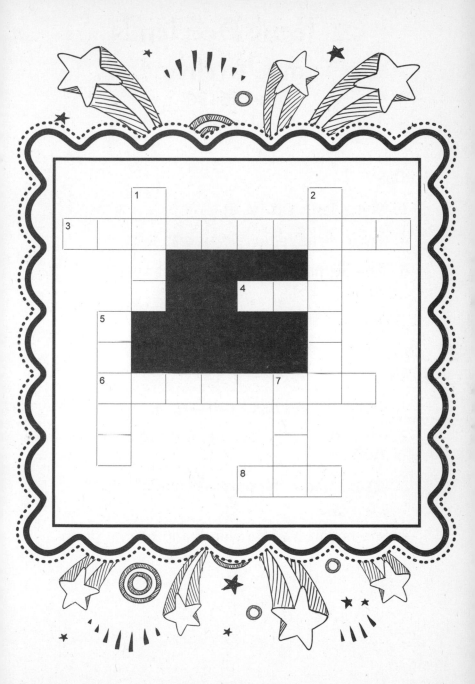

63. Jesus Befriends an Outcast
JOHN 4:5–30

ACROSS

   1. Where Jesus sat (v. 6)

   4. Name of the region Jesus was in (v. 5)

   6. Title of the person the outcast knew would come (v. 25)

   7. Depth of the well (v. 11)

DOWN

   1. Person Jesus talked with (v. 7)

   2. Name of person the well was named after (v. 6)

   3. Jesus offered the outcast "living" what? (v. 10)

   5. Son of Jacob who owned land nearby (v. 5)

133

64. Jesus Raises a Friend from the Dead

John 11:14-44

ACROSS

1. Jesus called Himself the resurrection and what else? (v. 25)

5. Name of the dead man (v. 14)

6. Place where the grave was (v. 38)

7. "Thy brother shall rise _____" (v. 23)

8. What is seen if one believes (v. 40)

DOWN

2. Number of days the man was dead (v. 39)

3. The command Jesus gave for the stone:
   "_____ ye _____" (v. 39)

4. What Jesus saw people doing (v. 33)

65. A Powerful Example
JOHN 13:1–14

ACROSS

    2. What the Teacher poured water into (v. 5)

    3. Part of the disciples that the Teacher washed (v. 5)

    4. Name of the man who would betray the Teacher (v. 2)

    6. Name of the feast in this Bible passage (v. 1)

DOWN

    1. Cloth the Teacher used in this example (v. 4)

    2. What Judas planned to do to the Teacher (v. 2)

    4. The person who set this example (v. 8)

    5. Who entered the heart of Judas Iscariot? (v. 2)

66. Jesus Comforts His Troubled Disciples

JOHN 14:1-7

Let not your **heart** be **troubled**: ye believe in God, believe also in me. In my **Father's** house are many mansions: if it were not so, I would have told you. I go to **prepare** a **place** for you. And if I go and prepare a place for you, I will **come** again, and **receive** you unto myself; that where I am, there ye may be also. And whither I go ye know, and the way ye know. **Thomas** saith unto him, Lord, we know not whither thou goest; and how can we know the way? Jesus saith unto him, I am the **way**, the **truth**, and the **life**: no man cometh unto the Father, but by **me**. If ye had known me, ye should have known my Father also: and from henceforth ye know him, and have seen him.

```
R E C E I V E S A T
A T P H E A R T I E
W E R T Y E U I O P
T R E U H T I W A Y
M K P T T G F D S A
E J A B H H C Q L I
E F R O O O M I E
T E E Y H T M N F F
U W P L A C E A E E
D E L B U O R T S B
```

Bonus Trivia!

What kind of contest did Jacob have with God?

    a) a chess game
    b) a footrace
    c) a wrestling match
    d) a Bible drill

Answer: c) a wrestling match (Genesis 32:24, 30)

139

67. Palm Sunday
MARK 11:1–11

And when they came nigh to **Jerusalem**, unto Bethphage and **Bethany**, at the mount of **Olives**, he sendeth forth **two** of his disciples, And saith unto them, Go your way into the **village** over against you: and as soon as ye be entered into it, ye shall find a colt tied, whereon never man sat; loose him, and bring him. And if any man say unto you, Why do ye this? say ye that the Lord hath need of him; and straightway he will send him hither. And they went their way, and found the **colt** tied by the door without in a place where two ways met; and they loose him. And certain of them that stood there said unto them, What do ye, loosing the colt? And they said unto them even as Jesus had commanded: and they let them go. And they brought the colt to Jesus, and cast their garments on him; and he sat upon him. And many spread their garments in the way: and others cut down **branches** off the trees, and strawed them in the way. And they that went before, and they that followed, cried, saying, **Hosanna**; Blessed is he that cometh in the name of the Lord: Blessed be the kingdom of our father David, that cometh in the name of the Lord: Hosanna in the highest. And Jesus entered into Jerusalem, and into the **temple**: and when he had **looked** round about upon all things, and now the eventide was come, he went out unto Bethany with the twelve.

```
W R T B E T H A N Y
E S E V I L O I P T
G A X Q D T S A S E
A J E R U S A L E M
L R U K J Y N F D P
L A C I B N N K O L
I S E H C N A R B E
V S J R O O T X T B
O D E K O O L A W A
S C H O O L S T O T
```

68. The Lord's Supper
MARK 14:12–26

And the first day of **unleavened** bread, when they killed the passover, his disciples said unto him, Where wilt thou that we go and prepare that thou mayest eat the passover? And he sendeth forth two of his disciples, and saith unto them, Go ye into the **city**, and there shall meet you a man bearing a pitcher of **water**: **follow** him. And wheresoever he shall go in, say ye to the goodman of the house, The Master saith, Where is the guest chamber, where I shall eat the passover with my disciples? And he will shew you a large **<u>upper room</u>** furnished and prepared: there make ready for us. And his disciples went forth, and came into the city, and found as he had said unto them: and they made ready the **passover**. And in the evening he cometh with the twelve. And as they sat and did eat, Jesus said, Verily I say unto you, One of you which eateth with me shall **betray** me. And they began to be sorrowful, and to say unto him one by one, Is it I? and another said, Is it I? And he answered and said unto them, It is one of the twelve, that dippeth with me in the dish. The Son of man indeed goeth, as it is written of him: but woe to that man by whom the Son of man is betrayed! good were it for that man if he had never been born. And as they did eat, Jesus took **bread**, and blessed, and brake it, and gave to them, and said, Take, eat: this is **<u>my body</u>**. And he took the **cup**, and when he had given thanks, he gave it to them: and they all drank of it. And he said unto them, This is **<u>my blood</u>** of the new testament, which is shed for many. Verily I say unto you, I will drink no more of the fruit of the vine, until that day that I drink it new in the kingdom of God. And when they had sung an **hymn**, they went out into the mount of Olives.

```
A  P  P  A  S  S  O  V  E  R
L  K  J  H  G  F  D  S  W  M
I  M  Y  B  O  D  Y  A  C  O
H  Y  M  N  R  T  T  M  B  O
U  B  Y  V  I  E  T  A  E  R
M  L  B  C  R  C  A  V  T  R
F  O  L  L  O  W  I  D  R  E
B  O  P  U  C  H  G  U  A  P
C  D  M  N  B  V  C  X  Y  P
D  E  N  E  V  A  E  L  N  U
```

69. Garden of Gethsemane
LUKE 22:39–46

And he came out, and went, as he was wont, to the **mount** of **Olives**; and his disciples also followed him. And when he was at the place, he said unto them, Pray that ye enter not into temptation. And he was withdrawn from them about a stone's cast, and kneeled down, and **prayed**, saying, Father, if thou be willing, remove this cup from me: nevertheless <u>**not my will**</u>, but thine, be done. And there appeared an **angel** unto him from heaven, strengthening him. And being in an agony he prayed more earnestly: and his **sweat** was as it were great **drops** of **blood** falling down to the **ground**. And when he rose up from prayer, and was come to his disciples, he found them sleeping for **sorrow**, And said unto them, Why sleep ye? rise and pray, lest ye enter into temptation.

```
A  S  D  F  G  P  H  J  K  L
P  O  I  U  D  R  O  P  S  W
Q  C  M  B  A  A  J  K  Y  O
U  N  O  T  M  Y  W  I  L  L
Y  S  U  N  D  E  F  I  E  G
T  U  N  C  X  D  V  Z  G  R
A  S  T  E  D  E  M  A  N  O
E  E  J  P  S  O  R  E  A  U
W  J  D  O  O  L  B  K  B  N
S  O  R  R  O  W  N  O  C  D
```

Bonus Trivia!

What was Samson famous for?

    a) skateboarding skills

    b) great strength

    c) musical talent

    d) writing poems

Answer: b) great strength (Judges 16:6)

70. A Rooster Crows
Matthew 26:69–75

Now **Peter** sat without in the palace: and a damsel came unto him, saying, Thou also wast with Jesus of **Galilee**. But he **denied** before them all, saying, I know not what thou sayest. And when he was gone out into the porch, another maid saw him, and said unto them that were there, This fellow was also with Jesus of **Nazareth**. And **again** he denied with an **oath**, I do not know the man. And after a while came unto him they that stood by, and said to Peter, Surely thou also art one of them; for thy speech bewrayeth thee. Then began he to curse and to swear, saying, I know not the man. And immediately the cock crew. And Peter **remembered** the **word** of Jesus, which said unto him, Before the cock **crow**, thou shalt deny me thrice. And he went out, and **wept** bitterly.

```
R E M E M B E R E D
H A N M X E V R E M
T T D R O W E P T P
A C E Q O I U Y T E
O P S R A S D F G T
R A C G A L I L E E
E G H A T Z Y X W R
J A B C Y E A J I V
A I V U D E I N E D
M N B V C X Z L K J
```

 Bonus Trivia!

What idol did Moses' brother, Aaron, create for the people of Israel?

- a) the Golden Bull
- b) the Golden Eagle
- c) the Golden Calf
- d) the Golden Arches

Answer: c) the Golden Calf (Exodus 32:3–4)

71. Barabbas Gets Freedom—Jesus Gets Death

Mark 15:6–14

Now at that feast he released unto them one **prisoner**, whomsoever they desired. And there was one named **Barabbas**, which lay bound with them that had made insurrection with him, who had committed **murder** in the insurrection. And the multitude crying aloud began to desire him to do as he had ever done unto them. But **Pilate** answered them, saying, Will ye that I release unto you the **King** of the **Jews**? For he knew that the **chief** priests had delivered him for **envy**. But the chief priests moved the people, that he should rather **release** Barabbas unto them. And Pilate answered and said again unto them, What will ye then that I shall do unto him whom ye call the King of the Jews? And they cried out again, Crucify him. Then Pilate said unto them, Why, what evil hath he done? And they cried out the more exceedingly, **Crucify** him.

```
I  N  P  R  I  S  O  N  E  R
K  P  S  I  E  O  N  C  S  S
I  Y  D  C  X  L  R  B  A  A
N  V  Q  S  R  U  E  B  S  U
G  N  W  P  C  S  B  A  B  A
O  E  Y  I  G  A  H  U  S  T
J  A  F  L  R  P  O  R  T  E
X  Y  S  A  T  C  H  I  E  F
A  C  B  T  A  S  D  F  G  H
V  U  R  E  D  R  U  M  J  K
```

72. Jesus Killed!

John 19:17–27

ACROSS

2. Jesus said Mary would now be this to His favorite disciple (v. 27)

4. Hebrew word for place where Jesus was killed (v. 17)

5. What was done to Jesus and others (v. 18)

7. "The place of a _____" (v. 17)

8. One of the three languages on sign on Jesus' cross (v. 20)

DOWN

1. The person who wrote the sign on the cross (v. 19)

3. Number of criminals killed along with Jesus (v. 18)

6. How many parts did the soldiers divide Jesus' garments into? (v. 23)

7. Jesus said His favorite disciple would now be this to Mary (v. 26)

73. Jesus Buried
John 19:38-42

And after this **Joseph** of Arimathaea, being a **disciple** of Jesus, but **secretly** for fear of the Jews, besought Pilate that he might take away the body of Jesus: and Pilate gave him leave. He came therefore, and took the body of Jesus. And there came also **Nicodemus**, which at the first came to Jesus by **night**, and brought a **mixture** of **myrrh** and **aloes**, about an hundred pound weight. Then took they the **body** of Jesus, and wound it in linen clothes with the **spices**, as the manner of the Jews is to bury. Now in the place where he was crucified there was a **garden**; and in the garden a **new** sepulchre, wherein was never man yet laid. There laid they Jesus therefore because of the Jews' preparation day; for the sepulchre was nigh at hand.

```
A S D F G H J K L P
M N I C O D E M U S
D I S C I P L E S N
J G Q M I X T U R E
O H J Y N Z W Y R D
S T S R W E D R A R
E D E R A O W O W A
P G O H B S R E C G
H Y L T E R C E S A
F Z A P S P I C E S
```

What kind of animal tempted Eve to eat the fruit that God said she should not eat?

    a) serpent

    b) hawk

    c) horse

    d) hippopotamus

Answer: a) serpent (Genesis 3:1–5)

74. Resurrection!
LUKE 24:1–9

Now upon the **first** day of the week, **very early** in the **morning**, they came unto the sepulchre, bringing the spices which they had prepared, and certain others with them. And they found the **stone** rolled **away** from the sepulchre. And they entered in, and found not the body of the Lord Jesus. And it came to pass, as they were much perplexed thereabout, behold, two men stood by them in shining garments: And as they were afraid, and bowed down their faces to the earth, they said unto them, Why seek ye the **living** among the **dead**? He is **not** here, but **is risen**: remember how he spake unto you when he was yet in Galilee, saying, The Son of man must be delivered into the hands of sinful men, and be crucified, and the **third** day rise **again**. And they remembered his words, and returned from the sepulchre, and told all these things unto the **eleven**, and to all the rest.

```
T  S  R  I  F  A  S  D  F  G
A  G  A  I  N  A  W  A  Y  J
K  S  M  N  I  A  Y  L  C  T
G  T  T  O  D  X  R  H  I  H
N  O  N  B  R  A  D  E  C  I
I  N  D  A  E  N  E  P  O  R
V  E  E  Y  V  D  I  D  S  D
I  S  R  I  S  E  N  N  M  R
L  E  L  E  V  E  N  O  G  A
V  B  N  M  L  K  J  H  T  G
```

75. Mary's Grief Turned to Joy
JOHN 20:11–18

But Mary stood without at the sepulchre weeping: and as she **wept**, she stooped down, and looked into the sepulchre, and seeth **two** angels in **white** sitting, the one at the **head**, and the other at the feet, where the body of Jesus had lain. And they say unto her, Woman, why weepest thou? She saith unto them, Because they have taken away my Lord, and I know not where they have laid him. And when she had thus said, she turned herself back, and saw Jesus standing, and knew not that it was Jesus. Jesus saith unto her, Woman, why weepest thou? whom seekest thou? She, supposing him to be the **gardener**, saith unto him, Sir, if thou have borne him hence, tell me where thou hast laid him, and I will take him away. **Jesus** saith unto her, **Mary**. She turned herself, and saith unto him, **Rabboni**; which is to say, **Master**. Jesus saith unto her, Touch me not; for I am not yet ascended to my Father: but go to my brethren, and say unto them, I ascend unto my Father, and your **Father**; and to my God, and your **God**. Mary Magdalene came and told the disciples that she had seen the **Lord**, and that he had spoken these things unto her.

M F A T H E R K O I
W H J E S U S N B R
J H E A D U Y G E V
C F I R T R D N X Z
M S O T E W E P T W
A L Q Y E D C V W F
S T Y R R H N M O J
T U R A B B O N I D
E I G M K L O P O Q
R A Z X S W E G D C

76. Ascension
Acts 1:3–11

To whom also he shewed himself alive after his passion by many infallible proofs, being seen of them **forty** days, and speaking of the things pertaining to the kingdom of God: And, being assembled together with them, commanded them that they should not depart from Jerusalem, but wait for the promise of the Father, which, saith he, ye have heard of me. For John truly baptized with water; but ye shall be **baptized** with the Holy Ghost not many days hence. When they therefore were come together, they asked of him, saying, Lord, wilt thou at this time restore again the kingdom to Israel? And he said unto them, It is not for you to know the times or the seasons, which the Father hath put in his own **power**. But ye shall receive power, after that the Holy Ghost is come upon you: and ye shall be witnesses unto me both in Jerusalem, and in all Judaea, and in Samaria, and unto the uttermost part of the earth. And when he had spoken these things, while they beheld, he was taken up; and a **cloud** received him out of their **sight**. And while they looked stedfastly toward heaven as he went up, behold, **two** men stood by them in **white** apparel; Which also said, Ye men of **Galilee**, why stand ye gazing up into heaven? this **same Jesus**, which is **taken up** from you into heaven, shall so **come** in like manner as ye have seen him go into heaven.

O	P	I	U	Y	T	R	W	E	Q
F	O	R	T	Y	S	H	W	S	A
G	W	D	E	Z	I	T	P	A	B
A	E	A	Z	T	X	T	U	M	I
L	R	I	E	W	U	C	N	E	B
I	T	B	C	O	M	E	E	J	L
L	G	H	L	K	J	H	K	E	E
E	P	J	G	V	O	W	A	S	R
E	R	T	I	I	Y	E	T	U	A
C	L	O	U	D	S	R	O	S	D

77. The Birth of the Church
Acts 2:1–8

ACROSS

2. What the believers thought they heard (v. 2)

3. The special day the believers were together (v. 1)

6. This came from heaven (v. 2)

8. How the event occurred (v. 2)

9. Who enabled the believers to speak in other languages? (v. 4)

DOWN

1. What appeared above each of the believers? (v. 3)

4. "And there appeared unto them cloven _____" (v. 3)

5. In whose tongue and language did each person hear? (v. 6)

6. The first thing the believers did when filled with the Holy Ghost (v. 4)

7. How many were filled with the Holy Ghost? (v. 4)

78. Dorcas Restored to Life
Acts 9:36–42

Now there was at Joppa a certain disciple named **Tabitha**, which by interpretation is called **Dorcas**: this woman was full of good works and almsdeeds which she did. And it came to pass in those days, that she was **sick**, and **died**: whom when they had washed, they laid her in an upper chamber. And forasmuch as Lydda was nigh to **Joppa**, and the disciples had heard that Peter was there, they sent unto him **two** men, desiring him that he would not delay to come to them. Then Peter arose and went with them. When he was come, they brought him into the upper chamber: and all the **widows** stood by him weeping, and shewing the coats and garments which Dorcas made, while she was with them. But **Peter** put them all forth, and kneeled down, and **prayed**; and turning him to the body said, Tabitha, arise. And she opened her **eyes**: and when she saw Peter, she **sat** up. And he gave her his hand, and lifted her up, and when he had called the saints and widows, presented her **alive**. And it was known throughout all Joppa; and many believed in the Lord.

```
P  W  S  B  A  L  I  V  E  W
O  I  D  P  V  I  D  T  G  S
I  D  P  N  E  K  U  I  B  X
U  O  F  T  C  T  W  O  E  C
J  W  A  M  X  L  E  Y  V  D
Y  S  E  Y  E  O  J  R  F  O
T  A  G  L  Z  P  K  H  R  R
R  Q  H  K  R  E  C  N  E  C
E  W  J  T  A  B  I  T  H  A
P  R  A  Y  E  D  S  M  D  S
```

79. Rhoda's Blooper
Acts 12:11–17

And when **Peter** was come to himself, he said, Now I know of a surety, that the Lord hath **sent** his **angel**, and hath delivered me out of the hand of Herod, and from all the expectation of the people of the Jews. And when he had considered the thing, he came to the house of **Mary** the mother of John, whose surname was Mark; where many were gathered together **praying**. And as Peter **knocked** at the **door** of the gate, a damsel came to hearken, named **Rhoda**. And when she knew Peter's **voice**, she opened not the gate for gladness, but ran in, and told how Peter stood before the gate. And they said unto her, Thou art **mad**. But she constantly affirmed that it was even so. Then said they, It is his angel. But Peter continued knocking: and when they had opened the door, and saw him, they were **astonished**. But he, beckoning unto them with the hand to hold their peace, declared unto them how the Lord had brought him out of the **prison**. And he said, Go shew these things unto James, and to the brethren. And he departed, and went into another place.

```
L P R A Y I N G X D
K H U R V O I C E E
J G I Y E Q M H S K
N F O T W T S E W C
O M A R Y I E D L O
S D P H N Z N P O N
I R O O D X T C M K
R S T D E M N T J Q
P S A A R C A G U A
A N G E L V B D B Z
```

80. Businesswoman Believer
Acts 16:14–15

And a certain woman named **Lydia**, a **seller** of
purple, of the city of **Thyatira**, which **worshipped**
God, heard us: whose heart the Lord **opened**,
that she attended unto the things which were
spoken of **Paul**. And when she was baptized, and
her household, she besought us, saying, If ye have
judged me to be **faithful** to the **Lord**, come into my
house, and **abide** there. And she constrained us.

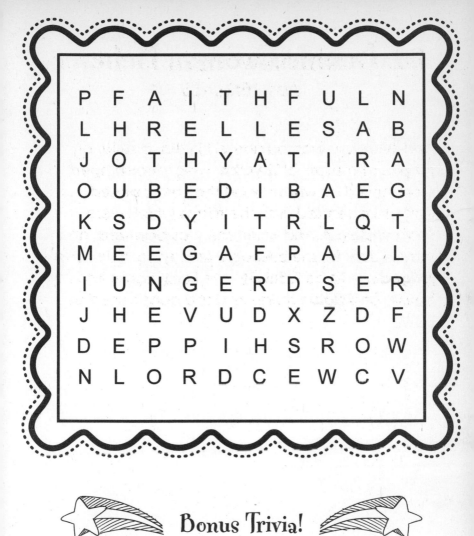

```
P F A I T H F U L N
L H R E L L E S A B
J O T H Y A T I R A
O U B E D I B A E G
K S D Y I T R L Q T
M E E G A F P A U L
I U N G E R D S E R
J H E V U D X Z D F
D E P P I H S R O W
N L O R D C E W C V
```

Bonus Trivia!

What did God put in the sky as a promise never again to destroy the earth with a flood?

    a) birds

    b) the moon

    c) a rainbow

    d) the space shuttle

81. Love Is Greater Than. . .
1 Corinthians 13:1–7

ACROSS

    2. What could be given to be burned (v. 3)

    4. What could be understood (v. 2)

    6. What men and angels could speak with (v. 1)

    8. What can move mountains (v. 2)

DOWN

    1. Who could be fed from our possessions (v. 3)

    3. Noisy musical instrument (v. 1)

    5. What we should rejoice in (v. 6)

    7. "Though I have the ___ of prophecy" (v. 2)

82. The Armor of God
EPHESIANS 6:14–18

Stand therefore, having your loins girt about with **truth**, and having on the breastplate of righteousness; and your **feet** shod with the preparation of the **gospel** of **peace**; above all, taking the **shield** of **faith**, wherewith ye shall be able to quench all the fiery darts of the wicked. And take the **helmet** of **salvation**, and the **sword** of the **Spirit**, which is the **word** of **God**: Praying always with all **prayer** and supplication in the Spirit, and watching thereunto with all perseverance and supplication for all saints.

```
S H I E L D E F S A
W A P G O S P E L O
O I L P R A Y E R X
R M C V E S A T O T
D R P E A C E F N D
H E L M E T R A E G
T W I T H T I A F O
U U K O A R W O R D
R S P I R I T J N U
T O R N A E S L P U
```

Bonus Trivia!

What was Saul looking for when he learned he would become the king of Israel?

    a) a wife
    b) lost donkeys
    c) water
    d) a job

Answer: b) lost donkeys (1 Samuel 10:1-2)

83. Timothy's Mom and Grandma

2 Timothy 1:3–7

I thank God, whom I serve from my forefathers with pure **conscience**, that without ceasing I have remembrance of thee in my **prayers** night and day; greatly **desiring** to see thee, being mindful of thy **tears**, that I may be filled with joy; when I call to remembrance the unfeigned **faith** that is in thee, which dwelt first in thy grandmother **Lois**, and thy mother **Eunice**; and I am persuaded that in thee also. Wherefore I put thee in remembrance that thou <u>stir up</u> the gift of God, which is in thee by the putting on of my **hands**. For God hath not given us the **spirit** of fear; but of **power**, and of **love**, and of a <u>sound mind</u>.

```
D E S I R I N G S E
K C U A S L A H R L
H N M N P S I O E O
A E F A I T H L Y V
N I M N R C N C A E
D C H O I T E A R S
S S B S T I R U P T
E N I C A L A I R N
S O U N D M I N D J
L C P O W E R L B Y
```

Bonus Trivia!

What did Jesus say little children should do?

    a) "Be quiet in church!"

    b) "Come to Me."

    c) "Read your Bibles."

    d) "Obey your parents."

Answer: b) "Come to Me" (Matthew 19:14)

84. Mighty Jesus
REVELATION 19:11–16

And I saw **heaven** opened, and behold a **white horse**; and he that sat upon him was called **Faithful** and True, and in righteousness he doth **judge** and make war. His eyes were as a flame of fire, and on his head were many **crowns**; and he had a name written, that no man knew, but he himself. And he was clothed with a vesture dipped in **blood**: and his name is called The **Word of God**. And the **armies** which were in heaven followed him upon white horses, clothed in fine linen, white and **clean**. And out of his mouth goeth a sharp **sword**, that with it he should smite the nations: and he shall **rule** them with a rod of iron: and he treadeth the winepress of the fierceness and **wrath** of Almighty God. And he hath on his vesture and on his thigh a name written, KING OF KINGS, AND LORD OF LORDS.

E F O C M L B T N E
W R A T H T L D S A
I C S I B S O R N J
A L E L T A O O W U
N E V A E H D W O D
E A H I E B F S R G
L N V T H S O U C E
X O I L N Y L E L J
K H R I S E I M R A
W O R D O F G O D Y

175

ANSWERS

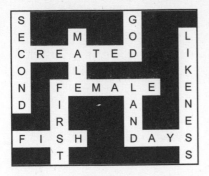

Puzzle 1

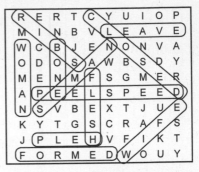

Puzzle 2

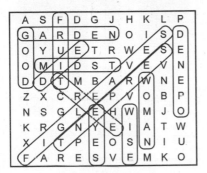

Puzzle 3

Puzzle 4

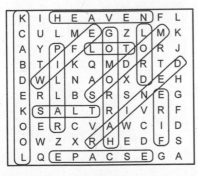

Puzzle 5

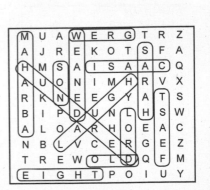

Puzzle 6

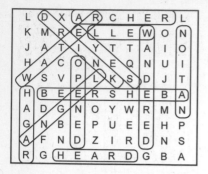

Puzzle 7

Puzzle 8

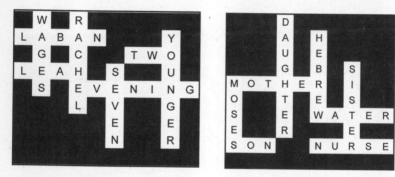

Puzzle 9

Puzzle 10

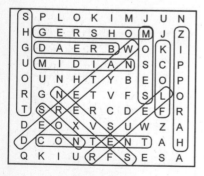

Puzzle 11

Puzzle 12

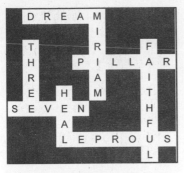

Puzzle 13

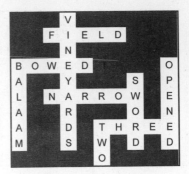

Puzzle 14

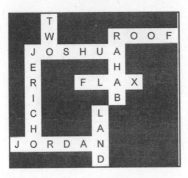

Puzzle 15

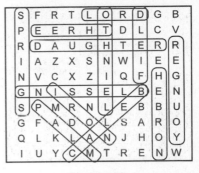

Puzzle 16

Puzzle 17

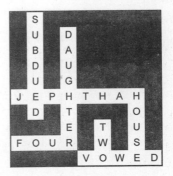

Puzzle 18

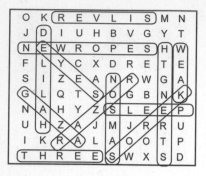

Puzzle 19

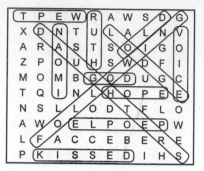

Puzzle 20

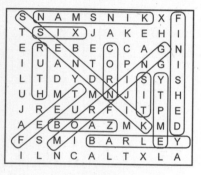

Puzzle 21

Puzzle 22

Puzzle 23

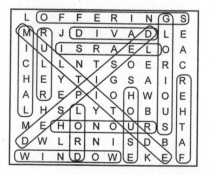

Puzzle 24

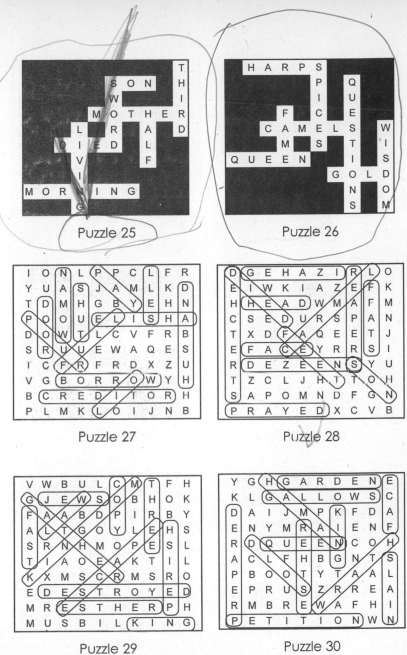

Puzzle 25

```
                    T
            S O N   H
          W         I
          M O T H E R
    L     R       A D
    I E D D       L
    I V           F
    I
M O R N I N G
    G
```

Puzzle 26

```
    H A R P S
    S P I C E S   Q
                  U
          F       E
          C A M E L S       W
          M       T         I
Q U E E N         I         S
                  O         D
            G O L D         O
                  N         M
                  S
```

Puzzle 27

```
I O N L P P C L   L   F R
Y U A   S J A M   L   K D
  D M   H G B Y   E   H H
P O O U E L I S   H A
D O W T L C V F   R   B
S R U U E W A Q   E   S
T C F R F R D X   Z   U H
V G B O R R O W   Y   Y H
B C R E D I T O R     H
P L M K L O I J N B
```

Puzzle 28

```
D G E H A Z I R   R   L O
E I W K I A Z E   E   F K
H H E A D W M A   F   A M
C S E D U R S P   A   T N J
T X D F A Q E E   T   S I
E R F A C E Y R   R   S U
R D E Z E E N S   Y
T Z C L J H T   T O N
S A P O M N D F   G
P R A Y E D X C V B
```

Puzzle 29

```
V W B U L C M T F H
G J E W S O B H O K
F A A B D P I R B Y
A L T G O Y L E H S
S R N H M O P E S L
T I A O E A K T I L
K X M S C R M S R O
E D E S T R O Y E D
M R E S T H E R P H
M U S B I L K I N G
```

Puzzle 30

```
Y G H G A R D E N E
K L G A L L O W S C
D A I J M P K F D A
E N Y M R A I E N F
R A D Q U E E N C O H
A C L F H B G N T S
P B O O T Y T A A L
E P R U S Z R R E A
R M B R E W A F H I
P E T I T I O N W N
```

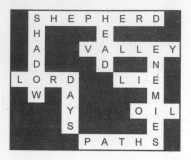

Puzzle 31

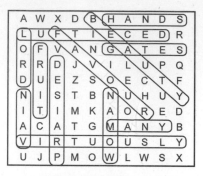

Puzzle 32

Puzzle 33

Puzzle 34

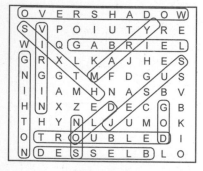

Puzzle 35

Puzzle 36

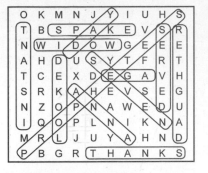

Puzzle 37

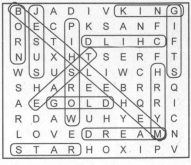

Puzzle 38

Puzzle 39

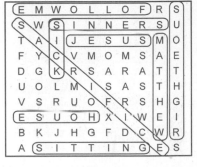

Puzzle 40

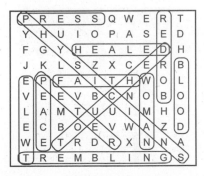

Puzzle 41

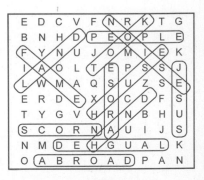

Puzzle 42

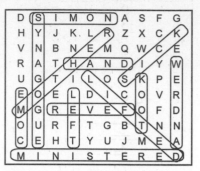

Puzzle 43

Puzzle 44

Puzzle 45

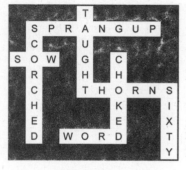

Puzzle 46

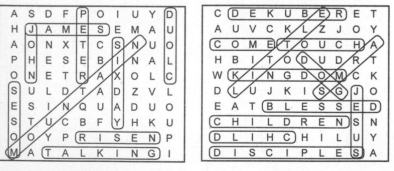

Puzzle 47

Puzzle 48

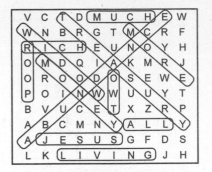

Puzzle 49

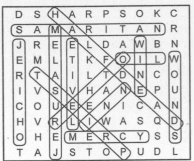

Puzzle 50

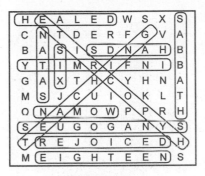

Puzzle 51

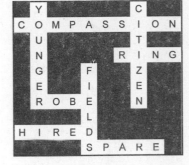

Puzzle 52

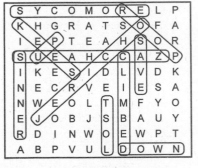

Puzzle 53

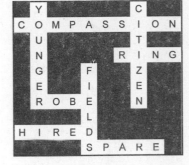

Puzzle 54

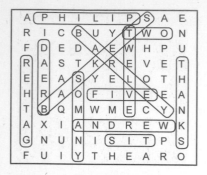

Puzzle 55

Puzzle 56

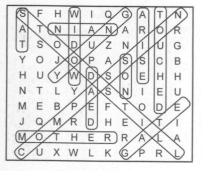

Puzzle 57

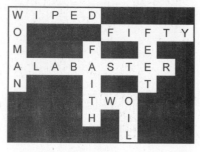

Puzzle 58

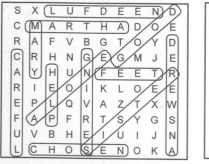

Puzzle 59

Puzzle 60

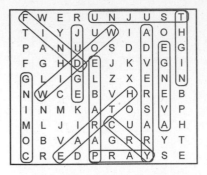

Puzzle 61

Puzzle 62

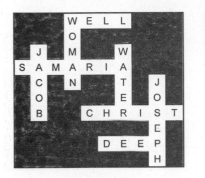

Puzzle 63

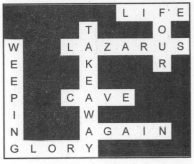

Puzzle 64

Puzzle 65

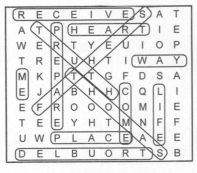

Puzzle 66

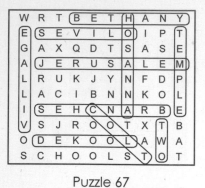

Puzzle 67

```
P A S S O V E R
A P P A S S O V E R R
L K J H G F D S W M M
I M Y B O D Y A C O O
H Y M N R T T M B E O
U B Y V I E T A E R R
M L B C R C A V T R R
F O L L O W I D R E E
B O P U C H G U A P P
C D M N B V C X Y P P
D E N E V A E L N U U
```

Puzzle 68

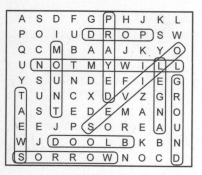

Puzzle 69

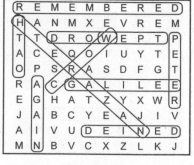

Puzzle 70

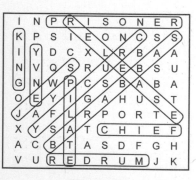

Puzzle 71

Puzzle 72

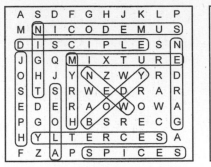

Puzzle 73

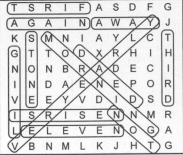

Puzzle 74

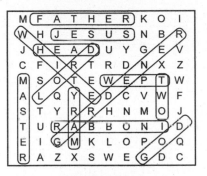

Puzzle 75

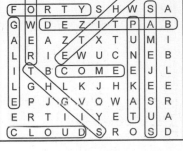

Puzzle 76

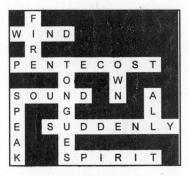

Puzzle 77

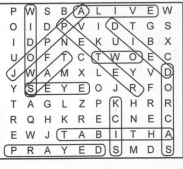

Puzzle 78

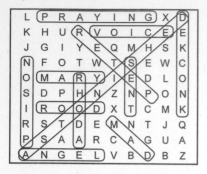

Puzzle 79

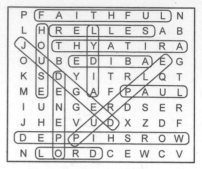

Puzzle 80

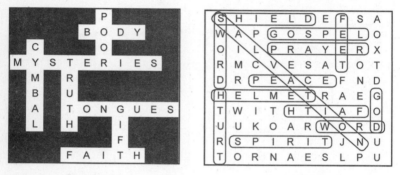

Puzzle 81

Puzzle 82

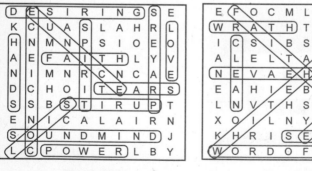

Puzzle 83

Puzzle 84

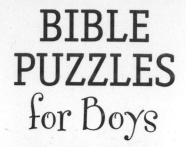
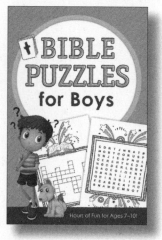